The Female Assumption

The Female Assumption

*A Mother's Story: Freeing Women from
the View that Motherhood is a Mandate*

Melanie Holmes

Melanie Holmes website: http://www.melanieholmesauthor.com

FIRST EDITION

Library of Congress Cataloging-in-Publication Data

Holmes, Melanie
The Female Assumption: A Mother's Story, Freeing Women From the View that Motherhood is a Mandate/Melanie Holmes – 1st ed.

ISBN-13: 978-1500933050
ISBN-10: 1500933058

1. Holmes, Melanie.   2. Women's Lives   3. Motherhood
4. Childless Childfree

For my daughter

TABLE OF CONTENTS

Endorsements

"As a woman who chose to arrive at motherhood later in life, I shared (and continue to share) many of the perspectives that Melanie Holmes brings to light in *The Female Assumption*. Motherhood in our society continues to be thrust upon women as a salve to our own individual search for meaning, purpose, and legacy, and Holmes offers aspiring mothers a revealing analysis of the institution of motherhood they will surely benefit from when making the decision."

- Lisa Haisha, Life Coach, Women's Advocate, Author, and Founder of Soul Blazing Sanctuary

"Melanie Holmes has done something that few people dare to do: question the assumption that all women should have children. She draws from history, literature, and her own research to knock down conventional wisdom. She's opening up space for each woman to decide for herself the way forward, whatever that may be, and that's a great service."

- Lisa Hymas, Senior Editor and Co-Founder of Grist.org

"The Female Assumption is an important and long overdue addition to the cultural dialogue around "motherhood or not" that our generation is beginning to engage in. As someone who has broken the taboo of talking about life after unchosen-childlessness not as a wasteland, but as an unexpectedly rich territory awaiting exploration, I really appreciate Holmes's courage in breaking the silence that surrounds the reality of modern mothering. With motherhood being touted as "the most meaningful thing a woman can do with her life" (a mantra of Motherhood Catechism as Holmes names it), it therefore follows that

her openness may cause some to call her a bad mother for spilling the beans, perhaps without actually reading this carefully researched, measured, loving, and thoughtful book. Holmes has taken a hefty swing at the myths of motherhood and I'm very grateful to her for doing so. I'm sure many other childless women will be too."
  - Jody Day, Author and Founder of Gateway Women

"I love this book! The is an oft debated question, but it comes and goes, especially as young women have been again led to believe in the myth that you can have it all, juggling children, jobs, etc. I am 61, happily never married and have no children. These were conscious choices."
  - Dr. Julianne Malveaux, President/Founder,
  Economic Education & J.M. Malveaux Enterprises

Acknowledgments

I had a burning desire to write this book for years, but I wasn't sure how to put my thoughts into words. Listening to Dr. Patricia O'Brien speak about the experience of females in America, I heard the first hint of the words I had been struggling to find. She broadened my perspectives and helped me with the long birthing process that resulted in this book.

My husband listened to me for perhaps hundreds of hours on the topics herein. Without his support, I would have given up this dream before it began.

My children. For teaching me while I was teaching them. And for allowing me to use them as examples for the world to see.

Madelyn Cain, your openness to take on this topic when the 21st century was just dawning has inspired many, and will continue to do so as the conversation amplifies. I am humbled by your support. My gratitude and respect is boundless.

My earliest "free" editors: you know who you are; thank you for encouraging and challenging me. Your early participation helped me create a product that was worthy of moving forward to the professional realm. And to my later "free" editors: my profound thanks in helping me polish, punctuate, and prime my copy for publication.

My Editor, Cindy DiTiberio, to whom I owe a great debt of gratitude for her wisdom in helping me to hone my message, and for her insightful analogy that publishing a book is like riding a roller coaster. Thank you, Cindy, for being one of the first "ups" on my ride and for believing in a first-time author. My agent, Beth Davey, for her unwavering support in the face of the "downs" of publishing. Beth, thank you for sticking by my side through so much.

To all those who came into my life during my research and writing, thank you for the investment of your time in this topic, for your advice, and your encouragement. Andrea Barzvi, thank you for urging me to dig deeper in the initial stages of my publishing journey.

To the 200 women who opened up their lives and hearts to me, including those who helped me reach them; thank you. I hope you are proud of what you helped create.

Thanks also to all who pick up this book in an effort to broaden your knowledge about the female experience: may life bring you much peace.

Melanie Holmes

Foreword by Madelyn Cain
Author of *The Childless Revolution: What it Means to be Childless Today*

Motherhood is important, powerful, draining and demanding, and not everyone is up to the task. It is a lifelong journey not to be entered into lightly. So why do so many women assume the role ignorant of the reality? Because no one has told them the truth. Instead, women are offered maxims about how they'll love it, how good they'll be at it, and how they'd better 'get on it' before it's too late. Thank goodness Melanie Holmes came along and assumed the position of tribal leader, initiating the next generation in what really lies ahead.

Holmes's goal is not to frighten but to enlighten. She wants women to explore all their reproduction avenues (including childlessness) with an open mind and armed with truth, not fantasy. She also wants a society that gives wide berth to women so they can make individual choices based on their own individual needs. Holmes wants women to know both sides of the reproduction coin so they don't merely toss that coin but plunk it down on the side they prefer, regardless of societal or parental pressures on them to procreate.

The Female Assumption is the first book to pull back the curtain of the nursery and show the true complexity of the mothering choice. Jennifer Senior in her book, *All Joy and No Fun,* says, "There's the parenting life of our fantasies and there's the parenting life of our banal, on-the-ground realities." In The New York Times, journalist Ross Douthat outs himself as a whiner now that he's become a father. "…a not-so-quiet desperation can seem pervasive among parents and it's worth it to try and understand why." Holmes takes on the task of explaining why and goes much further. (Read her "Dirty Little Secrets" in Chapter 4 and you'll have a much better idea about what Senior and Douthat are hinting at.)

Holmes's excellent book provides women with a raw look at mothering as well as a thorough examination of those who are childfree. This in-depth critical analysis is a gift to young women on the brink of making this life-altering decision who want to know what they might be in for.

The true aim of the Women's Liberation Movement is to give women the freedom to be who they wish to be. In this book, Holmes carries the torch and passes it on to the next generation.

Note: Madelyn Cain published *The Childless Revolution* in 2001 when her own daughter was 15. (Published by Perseus Publishing)

"If there's a book that you want to read, but it hasn't been written yet, then you must write it."
Toni Morrison, author

Preface

My biggest fear is that those I love the most will read this book and translate its contents into regret. With every ounce of my being, I want to make it clear that what is contained herein should *not* be interpreted as regret. For to regret the path I've traversed over the past three decades is to regret three beautiful souls who came into my life. My two sons and my daughter.

Despite the challenges that have accompanied my motherhood journey, I recognize the growth that I have experienced and I treasure the love that has come my way.

Motherhood is not usually described in all its layers of reality for the very reason that constitutes my own fear; that others may interpret regret. Often, women embark on the longest journey of their lives, traveling to an unknown destination, and only once they arrive do they learn about the place where they find themselves. The fact that the destination does not deliver all that the "motherhood travel guide" suggests does not hit home until later. The road is much harder and bumpier than most females ever suspect. It is my hope to present the challenges of motherhood here, so that women can take stock and evaluate whether motherhood is a destination that they desire.

Despite all the advances for women in the last few decades, we still, as a society, assume motherhood is the ultimate goal for females. Without realizing that perhaps not all females will want to, should, or be able to become moms, the message that the majority of females still hear is that motherhood is integral to a well-rounded life. These messages spring forth from varied sources and are ingrained into females' psyches. It is understandable, therefore, that many women pursue motherhood despite some really tough circumstances.

A friend of mine asked, "But what about the good things about being a mom? Don't we owe it to our daughters to encourage them to experience all the wonderful things about being a mother?" My answer: I would like to share as much information as possible with my daughter; I want her to feel encouraged no matter which direction her life takes. Talking about the joys of motherhood and leaving out the sacrifices leaves females unprepared for the life-long journey they will travel if they choose the motherhood path. If my daughter chooses motherhood, great! She'll get to experience some of what I've experienced. And if she opts out of motherhood, great! She'll get to experience a whole lot that I did not.

For those of us who are mothers, do we feel that our own choices would be diminished if our daughters do not follow in our footsteps by becoming mothers someday? Is there a sense of validation if our child wants what we wanted? Perhaps the mothers of the 1960s and '70s felt a diminishment of their lifestyle as women's rights took center stage and their daughters began putting off marriage, using birth control, and pursuing higher education and careers. As society evolves, our expectations for females' lives must evolve also.

So much about being a mom has changed since the days when I grew up. A child of the 1960s, the majority of the homes I observed consisted of the traditional family form with a mom, dad, and kids. Over the past few decades, motherhood has evolved from a parenting partnership to record numbers of single moms who carry the load of children, job, and everything else that comes their way. Some of this is due to the general acceptance of casual sex between consenting adults which often results in pregnancy. Back in what we might refer to as the "old days" (just a few decades ago), it was assumed that if a single female was pregnant, the father would step up to the marriage altar and do what was considered the right thing. Today, women can be in the workforce, often command good salaries, are independent, and no longer need a husband for financial support. We also see a high number of divorces, which leaves moms on their own, or at least experiencing motherhood in a very different way than they may have expected when they started out on the journey.

What has gotten lost in the equation is the necessary support system for mother and child that leads to the best possible circumstances for raising a child. It no longer seems that there is recognition of the importance of a parenting partnership (or support network) with which to raise children. In this book, you'll see that the partnership does not have to be the traditional form of husband/wife or mother/father. But a support system that is dependable and invested in the child's future ensures ample resources (emotional, financial, etc.) for the child and a much more balanced life for the mother.

Virginia Woolf wrote, "When a subject is highly controversial, one cannot hope to tell the truth. One can only show how one came to hold whatever opinion one does hold." This is what I plan to do.

In this book, I will demonstrate why I believe that females should be raised hearing that motherhood is only one option out of many paths they might choose in order to live a full, happy life. I will also demonstrate why I believe that the assumption that all women desire motherhood unknowingly narrows their menu of life choices, and in some cases, can do harm to the inner selves of females. It is up to us, as a society, to ensure that females are not set up for feelings of confusion, inadequacy, anger, or depression if they do not want or are unable to achieve motherhood. We can do this by refraining from assumptions about what their lives "should" look like.

I present several snapshots of motherhood in an attempt to dispel the belief that procreation is the yellow brick road to happiness. My attempt to expose motherhood may ultimately fray the fabric of motherhood just a little. Without condemning motherhood as a valid life choice, I would like to realistically frame an institution as old as the stories of Cain and Abel. In doing so, I hope to amplify the conversation about what it means to be female–including the discussion of motherhood as a choice rather than a foregone conclusion. This conversation has been around before; in the days of Mary Wollstonecraft (late 1700s), Charlotte Perkins Gilman (late 1800s-early 1900s), Simone de Beauvoir (mid-20th century), Tillie Olsen, and others. However, in the words of writer and lecturer Stephanie Mills, "the topic keeps vanishing."

I hope my words may serve as a guide to women who try to realistically evaluate whether motherhood is the right path for them. My main goal for this book is to give all of us (parents, grandparents, teachers, co-workers, friends, and the media) reason to examine our assumptions and refrain from espousing the so-called "right" path to an authentic female life.

Part I

Great Expectations

"It is better to live your own destiny imperfectly
than to live someone else's life with perfection."
Virginia Woolf, author

Chapter 1: Recipe for Exhaustion

"Sometimes I think checking out would be okay. Truly, I
try so hard and I get so tired. I know in my heart that I
have a lot left to do in this world. I decided to have three
beautiful children and I owe it to them to be strong. But I
just get so tired. Why does no one see just how tired I
am?"

When I wrote the above entry in my diary, I was employed
full-time in a very stressful job, and married with three
children. Two grown sons (one still living at home) and a
12-year-old daughter (a newly-emerging woman replete
with breasts and backtalk). True to the sandwich
generation, I also had an 80-year-old mother whose
medical issues led to her being placed in a rehabilitation
facility; and the only way she could transition back to
living in her own home was if someone could spend 24/7
with her for a few weeks. Thus, I took a month off my job
so that I could help her get home. I was also taking two
night classes in order to finish a bachelor's degree I'd
started 20 years earlier. This meant driving 90 miles twice
a week for a month in the midst of a typical Chicago
winter, and arranging care for my mom while I was away.

To say that on March 28, 2010, I was thoroughly and
completely exhausted is an understatement. But here's the
thing: being exhausted has been the theme of my adult life.
And to what do I attribute it? The demands of everyday
life while filling so many roles, the most demanding role
being that of mother.

The beautiful title of Mother brings visions of heartfelt greeting cards and the sweet giggles of babes. That life-altering, all-encompassing title reflects a role revered by many. But there I was on the date in question, daydreaming about checking out because I was so completely burned out by all the responsibilities placed upon my shoulders. Mind you, I have three good kids. I haven't had the drama that many moms are faced with. Suffice it to say that my two sons completed high school relatively unscathed. My daughter is in high school and I'm keeping my fingers crossed for good results like those of her older brothers. Yes, all three of my kids have been "normal" kids, making "normal" mistakes, going through "normal" stages. And what I was feeling as a 48-year-old mother of three was normal too. Wait, did I just say it's normal to dream about the quietude of death as alluded to in my journal? Actually, that is exactly what I'm saying.

I am not here to throw a pity party for myself or any other mother. When I say that I attribute my exhaustion largely to motherhood, there is a huge difference between attribution and blame. I do not *blame* motherhood. I am simply describing a reality. To put it bluntly, motherhood is damn hard. That's a sentiment that won't sell many greeting cards.

When I think back to the 21-year-old me, I recall a person who did not think twice about having children. I was married, thus, I felt that the next logical step was having a baby. I remember feeling happy (and sleep deprived) as a new mom despite the fact that I had to work outside the home and leave my baby with a sitter. I cried all the way to work on the first day I dropped off my baby boy and boarded a commuter train for the city. It was the mid-1980s and the American economy was transitioning to a point where it was hard for just one breadwinner to support a family. At the same time, gender roles in the home were

4

still firmly entrenched. I felt the full load of responsibility with regard to child-rearing and housekeeping on top of my full-time job outside my home. After a significant medical issue and a second baby, my then-husband (now my ex-husband) and I found a way for me to quit my job. The ensuing few years found me alternately restless and contented. I knew what I was doing was important, but I felt a rising tide of restlessness as I tended the needs of highly-active toddlers.

Perhaps what I felt fits the description of Betty Friedan's "feminine mystique." I wasn't unhappy and I felt lucky to be able to be at home with my kids. However, women were entering college in increasing numbers in the 1980s and pursuing their own careers. The question women heard more often than in the previous decade was, "And what do you do?" I yearned for a role outside my home that would supply me with a ready answer to that inevitable question.

My own mother devoted many years at home caring for five children. I was two years old when my dad was permanently disabled, and my mom returned to the workforce. I don't remember any dialogue with my mom about the challenges, sacrifices, or heavy-lifting of motherhood. I guess you could say that my mom passed along the proverbial "rose-colored motherhood glasses" to me; the ones she received from her mother before her.

I, along with so many females, have been indoctrinated to be selfless and to think of myself as the water pitcher that fills up everyone else's glasses, leaving mine drained. The term "supermom" became a common buzzword in the late 20th century and is going strong as ever in the 21st century. Even though females are mere mortal beings, many moms *seem* as if they can do it all. *Seem* is the operative word in that sentence. I am one of those moms who *seem* to be able to do it all. I love my children with every ounce of my being and I'm there for them when they need me. It feels good when I can help them, and it is also tiring and draining. The latter part of that statement is not to be discussed in polite company. But it is time to shed some of the secrecy and paint motherhood in all its shades of reality—some good, some not-so-good, and some downright ugly.

As I contemplate the world in which my own daughter is growing up, I feel trepidation. In truth, my anxiety for my daughter began when she was in utero. This is because, by that time, I had amassed a rather large envelope of knowledge of what females are up against in American society. I knew that the supermom mentality causes females to run themselves ragged trying to do it all, be it all, and so many crash and burn. Literally.

Motherhood is a path that, once embarked upon, must be followed through to completion. There's no backtracking if you find that the peaks, valleys, and detours are not what you expected. Motherhood is very hard. So why is it that we assume that it is the "right" path for all females?

In this book, I am going to say some things that I wish I'd heard while growing into the woman that I am today. I especially plan to say these words to my daughter. In fact, I am dedicating this book to that blossoming young woman in my life. I will endeavor to inform my daughter of the realities of motherhood so that she can evaluate whether the experience is for her. And if motherhood feels right, then hopefully she will choose her steps wisely. And if motherhood is *not* something that feels right, I will encourage her to ignore the pressures that society places upon her shoulders and endeavor to be who *she* wants to be. I hope she will view her life as a smorgasbord of options. She needs to hear that her father and I have no assumptions for her life other than to become a fully-functional member of society, to be kind, and to follow whatever path feels right.

I wish for females everywhere to hear this kind of encouragement from their parents, extended family, and friends. Some women look at this support as a kind of permission to choose the life that feels authentic. Motherhood should not be treated as a mandate; something to be checked off the to-do list in order to be successful. Women are complete beings. Period.

Page intentionally left blank

"Each of us has an inner compass that helps us know where to go and what to do… The first problem for all of us, men and women, is not to learn, but to unlearn."
Gloria Steinem, author/activist

Chapter 2: Motherhood Catechism

Motherhood Catechism is a term I learned from Dr. Patricia O'Brien in a sociology class at St. Xavier University in Chicago. It refers to the schooling of females to assume that they will someday become mothers. This molding of the female psyche is so ingrained that our daughters and sisters grow up feeling incomplete unless they find a way to fulfill what they feel is their destiny; or rather, what society has *indoctrinated them* to feel is their destiny.

The thought that this kind of "fortune-telling" could be detrimental never occurs to the population at large. Educator and author Eda Leshan wrote, "One of the greatest gifts we can give today's children is to become their fortune-tellers…to tell them they are lovable and full of wondrous possibilities…that the process of growing up gives us greater self-confidence and many more options about what we want to be and do."

A popular scenario in American culture takes place when a woman is getting married and finds herself besieged by shouts at her bridal shower, "You have to break at least one ribbon!" which is supposed to signal the birth of at least one baby to the union. This implies that her choice to be a mom is assumed.

The pressure that is placed on females to bring forth life is extreme. A newly married couple gets bombarded from all angles. In my own Roman Catholic wedding ceremony, my second husband and I vowed before our family and friends to welcome children into our marriage despite our private agreement *not* to have any biological children together. (I already had two sons from my first marriage.) The Catholic religion dictates what kind of birth control is acceptable which amounts to…not much. My own father refused to agree to this kind of constraint with regard to family planning. Thus, he and my mother called off their wedding only to later elope and be married by the justice of the peace. As a result, my mother could not partake of a weekly religious rite (referred to as Holy Communion) for 36 ½ years of marriage until my father's death. Can you imagine having a weekly reminder for 36 ½ years of a decision as personal as family planning?

Without getting into the psychological debate of nature versus nurture, suffice it to say that girls are coached almost from birth to embrace motherhood. As little girls, dolls are put into our arms to cradle and we learn to be gentle and nurturing. My two sons also had access to a baby doll at a very young age, but social scripting did not support their pursuance of this role so they soon cast aside the doll for trucks and other "boy toys"–toys involving much noise, movement, and manipulation. Girls hear voiced assumptions such as, "Someday *when* you become a mom…" or "You're so good with kids, you'll make such a great mommy someday." Seemingly innocuous phrases such as these contribute to the indoctrination of females to believe that motherhood is a foregone conclusion rather than a carefully examined choice.

How often we hear about the loud ticking of a woman's biological clock. I once had a friend who, by her mid-30s, hadn't met Mr. Right. When at last she found love with a nice guy, she discovered that he never wanted to have kids, so she broke off the relationship. She walked away from a love that felt true because the thought of living her life without ever becoming a mother was too hard to imagine.

A decade went by before she fell in love again and was married. She is happy; and she is not a mother. One could argue that my friend had to follow her heart. She wanted children and she may have been miserable if she had married Mr. Right Number 1. But I have wondered, if not for her indoctrination into Motherhood Catechism, might she have been more apt to stay with the man she'd loved ten years earlier? Thankfully, she went on to find Mr. Right Number 2.

I had another friend who was happily married for several years when she asked me what I thought about the need for a child to complete a marriage. After having gone through a divorce, the ensuing single mom experience, and then re-marrying, only to enter a very challenging stepfamily situation, I decided to quote a statistic I heard (recent studies reflect the same statistic[1])–that childless couples have happier marriages than couples who opt for children. This couple did end up having a baby. Not too long after the baby's birth, their marriage dissolved. My friend said that becoming a father was too much for her husband, that it forced him to grow up. Although there was more at play in this particular relationship, I disagree with the implication that not wanting a child makes one childish. To the contrary, I know some exceptionally mature people who do *not* have children, and I know some equally immature people who *are* parents.

Because of the assumption that women will become mothers someday, married women without children are often bombarded with questions; finding themselves the subject of intense curiosity. It seems that we cannot, as a society, understand those who do *not* want to procreate. Marisha[*] is in her 40s, she's happily married, and she has no children. Marisha described her experience at a

---

[*] Name has been changed.

professional conference where she fell in with a group of a half-dozen women, and eventually the topic of conversation turned to the women's children. Marisha busied herself by checking emails on her phone, trying to exclude herself from the banter, until the women turned to her expectantly. When questioned, she matter-of-factly replied that she and her husband never had children; her statement garnered a visual grimace from one of the women. Later, Marisha was taken aback when this highly-educated woman, who was unknown to her before that day, became "caustic" toward her through various comments as well as inquiring into the origins of Marisha's ethnic name in a somewhat mocking manner. It was as though Marisha was unworthy of this woman's respect once her status as a nonmother was revealed.

In light of Marisha's example, it is understandable when one receives an unsolicited explanation from a perfect stranger regarding their status as "childless." Once, upon meeting an older, married man in a professional setting, we got on the subject of children and this man promptly shared that he and his wife were "unable to have children." I remember feeling amazed that this man felt compelled to explain such a personal matter to me. Receiving puzzled looks from people when they discover his childless state, he had learned to head off judgment at the pass.

The outgrowths of Motherhood Catechism are so pervasive in society that it is sometimes hard to pick them out because the cultural tenets are ingrained in our psyches. We often find ourselves espousing these "mantras," usually without true analysis of what we're saying. The mantras of Motherhood Catechism are the things we say about motherhood that support the dogma that it is the quintessential female experience.

For example, I once read a friend's social media posting that said, "I never knew love until I became a mother." That is a very sweet sentiment, but one I vehemently disagree with. A mother's love is beautiful and all-encompassing. The love I share with my husband is different, but it is most certainly *love*; a true expression of the respect, tenderness, and admiration we feel for each other. Then there's the love I feel for my siblings. When my brother died suddenly years ago, I felt a vast emptiness and remained in a depressive fog for a long time. I felt this because my love for my brother was real and unconditional. The love I feel for my own mother reaches deep into my soul. And the love I feel for childhood friends, whom I've loved since we were toddlers, is a love that runs through my very existence. For anyone who has loved and lost a pet, they will attest to that form of "true love." When my husband and I lost a cat to illness, it was the first time I saw my husband sob. Sob. This man stands 6'3" and is a rock, with a military background, and I'd known him for seven years by the time I saw him sob for the loss of our precious Bobby Jo. The only other time I saw this man sob was when his mom died. Two times in two decades.

No one type of love is superior to another; they are just different aspects of love. When we tout motherly love as supreme to all other forms of love, we do an injustice to a great number of females who are led to believe that they must achieve motherhood at all costs. When we speak of motherly love as being the one true form of love, we are contributing to the indoctrination of females into Motherhood Catechism.

Even in books that examine a woman's right to choose whether to become a mother, one can still find sentiments that sound like mantras of Motherhood Catechism. Jessica Valenti wrote in her book, *Why Have Kids?* that motherhood is "an incredible, unparalleled experience."[2]

Merriam-Webster defines the word "unparalleled" as having no equal or match. It is this kind of statement, spoken with emotion and the love felt for one's child, that leaves women without children feeling a bit left out and wanting. I might have made a statement such as this when I started on my motherhood journey. After all, I was indoctrinated into Motherhood Catechism as a young woman. Through decades of experiences, as well as my research and interviews, I've acquired a heightened sensitivity in how I think and speak about this topic. Valenti is a strong proponent for women's rights, as am I. This demonstrates how even the strongest of proponents can get carried away with the emotions evoked by one's child. Few people *intend* to contribute to the feeling of isolation that many women feel who live their lives without children. But it does happen and the repercussions can be precarious.

Melanie Notkin, author of *Otherhood: Modern Women Finding a New Kind of Happiness,* stated, "The truth about childlessness in America is that most (not all) women—and men—desire to be parents."[3] Notkin cited a CDC Report covering the fertility rates in women and men, aged 15 to 44, which indicated that only 14% of all childless women are voluntarily childless, leaving the remaining 86% of women involuntarily childless (due to biology or circumstance).[4] One must examine the validity of including 15 and 16-year-olds in a study that asks them to evaluate their desires for parenthood. According to Dr. Frances Jensen, pediatric neurologist and Chair of Neurology at the Perelman School of Medicine/University of Pennsylvania, "A crucial part of the brain—the frontal lobes—are not fully connected in the teenage brain...which is the part of the brain that says: 'Is this a good idea? What is the consequence of this action?'"[5] Thus, the biological "truth" is that the brains of 15 and 16-year-olds are not fully developed enough to evaluate the consequences of choosing parenthood as a life choice. What these teens are saying mirrors the assumptions of those around them.

In a poll I conducted with 100+ women who are mothers of daughters (from across the U.S.), 88% responded that they assume their daughters will become mothers someday. In many cases, these mothers had multiple daughters; one mother responded that she assumes all five of her daughters will become mothers someday. Despite these assumptions, only half the mothers I surveyed indicated that they would be disappointed or unhappy if their daughters opted out of motherhood. And only 42% said that they would voice their opinions in an attempt to urge their daughters toward motherhood if they heard them express disinterest or ambivalence. But the bottom line is, if their daughters said they didn't want to have kids, most moms would ask, "why not?" If females hear the question, "why not?" with regard to motherhood, then shouldn't they also hear "why?" when they announce that they want to become mothers?

In a small survey conducted at two Midwestern colleges, mainly consisting of young women and men at the beginning of their adult journeys, the results showed overwhelmingly that Motherhood Catechism exists among the next generation of "parental prospects."[6] The assumptions held are about hypothetical daughters; without knowing the personality, temperament, or interests of the person they speak of, they make assumptions about what any daughter of theirs would desire. One woman said, "It would make me sad if a daughter of mine didn't become a mother because being a mother is a great thing (according to my mom and what I've seen)…I think she would regret it later in life." And another similar response, "When I have a daughter, I would expect her to want to become a mother one day…and get so much more out of life…and I would communicate how I feel about it."

15

We cannot deny the impact of these assumptions that are passed down generation after generation.

Anthropologist Edward Hall developed the iceberg analogy to illustrate that some aspects of a culture are easily viewed or apparent, while other aspects are difficult to identify or understand. Applying the iceberg analogy to women's lives, we are only able to see what is above the water level– their external appearances (see Illustration 1). Below the water's surface lie the many sources that influence women's lives: from career aspirations and fertility to religion, resources, childhood experiences, etc. Settling at the bottom of the iceberg are the assumptions and expectations that females hear growing up. Could it be that most women grow up with the desire to become mothers someday because of the messages they internalize from family, friends, media, co-workers, and other sources of influence? What if females did *not* grow up with the mental image that motherhood is the quintessential female experience? Would we still see the same level of desires, as reported by the CDC fertility study–that "most" women desire to become mothers?

Women living their lives without children, for whatever reason, continue to be targets of intrusive questions from family members, friends, even perfect strangers. All this can lead to feelings of confusion, pain, and sometimes anger. Some distance themselves from family members or friends because they get tired of hearing the "mantras" of Motherhood Catechism. With childless/childfree women, the "mantras" include intrusive, presumptuous things that people say to or about women who are not mothers. Often, comments are uttered without realization of the hurtful or irritating effect they can have. Verna* described how co-workers and others who do not know her will ask, "How

---

* Name has been changed.

16

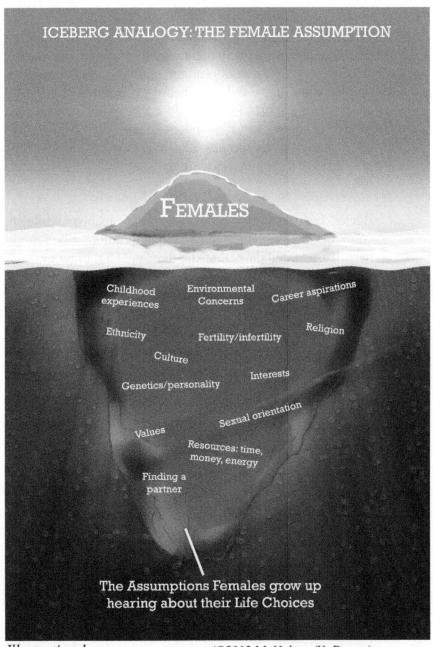

Illustration 1   (©2013 M. Holmes/K. Brown)

many kids do you have?" rather than "Do you have kids?" Verna recoils at this presumptuous question. This same line of questioning happened to another woman when she attended her high school reunion; and when she responded that she didn't have kids, she heard "Why not?" Most people may not mean to stereotype a woman with this type of inquiry. However, it is understandable how tiring it can be to deflect presumptuous questions on a regular basis, questions that crop up regularly over decades of a woman's life.

Becky* heard a mantra of Motherhood Catechism while she was working as a nanny to two small children. She found herself frustrated daily that she didn't get a moment to herself, "Even to go to the bathroom!" She was seriously questioning whether she wanted motherhood—ever. She called her mom and her mom replied, "It's different when they're your own." In truth, it's very much the same; as almost any mother will attest...time to yourself with small children underfoot? Not likely.

There is nothing wrong with veneration of motherhood; however, when it is touted as the toughest or most important job in the world—and the most rewarding—this too is a mantra of Motherhood Catechism. There are many tough and rewarding jobs. Children's cancer units are filled with people who perform heartwrenching jobs; and the medical researchers who have found treatments for various forms of cancer must revel in the rewards of knowing how many lives they will impact. From firefighters, police and military members to hospice workers, teachers, and leaders of the free world, these are all extremely important, tough, and impactful jobs.

---

* Names have been changed.

Gloria* talks with her daughters about future regret if they do not have children: "My daughters have an aunt who chose not to have children; she is almost 50 years old and regrets it." This statement evokes a vision of the stereotypical unhappy spinster and the forecast of a life spent in heartache if one follows in this woman's footsteps. Is it possible that this "unhappy aunt" expressed regret in a moment of sentimentality versus reality? Or that Gloria has inferred regret that may not actually exist?

An expression of regret *can be* another form of Motherhood Catechism, as demonstrated by the following interaction. Anne* told me, "My boss, who is also living her life happily without children, made the comment to a colleague who is a parent, 'I can hardly take care of myself,' when the topic of children came up...when I gently questioned her later, she said, 'Oh you know, you end up saying stupid things to justify your choice.'" Women without children have learned how to avoid these awkward confrontations by expressing regret when they don't really feel it because it's more socially acceptable.

Being prodded by so many in one's life can lead to anger, resentment, and sometimes, self-doubt. Hearing the statement, "My life was meaningless until I had kids," can have this effect. One woman related how, upon hearing this statement spoken by a celebrity, she reacted with self-doubt, even though she had already made peace with her life without children. She said that it gets so hard to shut out the plethora of messages that promote motherhood. Although a statement about life being meaningless without kids is myopic, it is often uttered without full realization of its connotation. Do we really believe that women without children lead lives devoid of meaning? Or that it is fair to devalue someone's existence based upon whether they

---

* Name has been changed.

choose to or are able to procreate? A mother's love for her child can lead her to say all kinds of wonderful things about motherhood; but it's important to remember that it is her own journey, and it's not for every woman.

Much like the celebrity's statement above, parents often claim that the birth of their child was the happiest moment of their lives, or what psychologist Abraham Maslow defined as "peak experiences... experiences of ecstasy, rapture, bliss."[7] Maslow describes peak experiences as being ego-transcending, affirming the meaning and value of existence, and leaving a permanent mark on the individual; as well as moments of inner peace, awe, and love. Undoubtedly, motherhood can bring with it moments of rapture. It also brings a purpose to one's everyday existence; keeping that little human being alive, healthy, and happy. But there are, in the words of Maslow, "thousands of descriptions of peak experiences."

Imagine the triumph of Nelson Mandela who went from prisoner to president of South Africa. Or Neil Armstrong's "giant leap for mankind" as he stepped onto the moon's surface. Or Marie Curie (a.k.a. Madame Curie), the first woman to receive a Nobel Peace Prize for her work in physics and chemistry, who changed the face of medicine and science.[8] When motherhood is described as *the* peak experience to trump all other peak experiences, doesn't it contribute to the feeling among women that motherhood is something they must achieve at all costs? How many other peak experiences must they give up in order to achieve this one?

The truth is that every door is open or ajar for women today; upon entering the door marked "motherhood," many other doors will inevitably close. We must free women from the mantras of Motherhood Catechism or we take the chance of urging females toward a door they might not want or are unable to open.

"Never limit yourself because of others' limited imaginations; never limit others because of your own limited imagination."
Mae Jemison, astronaut

Chapter 3: Evolution of Women's Choices in America

Women didn't always have a wide array of choices when it came to what path their life could take. In the United States, women's choices have been historically rooted in the domestic realm. Prior to the 20th century, women were not allowed to vote nor were they expected to pursue an education. Unfortunately, despite much progress, subjugation of females by their male counterparts is still entrenched in our culture—from politics to corporate ladders to religion. As of February 2014, twenty states had not sent a woman to the Senate and four states had not sent a woman to Congress.[1] Among Fortune 500 Companies, only 23 women have been appointed CEOs. And in major religions, women are still not allowed to be clergy, with no change in sight.

Dating back to the early part of the 1800s, women were treated like children without basic rights. Married, white women in the United States could not make wills, be the legal guardians of their children, nor own or inherit property. Think about that statement for a minute. Women could not be legal guardians of their own children. If a woman's husband died, the guardianship of her children would be transferred to a male family member of legal age. In essence, upon marriage a woman became the chattel property of her husband. The term "coverture" referred to women's legal subordinate status in marriage at that time. And the custom of a woman giving up her father's last name and taking on her husband's last name signified the transfer of her control from her father to her husband. In 1848, New York passed the Married Woman's Property

Act, after which the majority of the states passed similar laws over time.[2] Until then, a woman's property was under the control of her husband. This included *all* her property, even the clothes on her back. At the time, many objected to the Married Woman's Property Act on the basis that it was "anti-family." Throughout history, we see that the rights of women have been tightly tied to the institution of the family, which served to keep women firmly in their domestic role–caring for children and home. This happened with women's suffrage as well; with the public outcry against women's right to vote tied to fear that women would attend public meetings to hear candidates' views, thereby neglecting home, hearth, and children. In other words, the increase of women's stature was correlated with the demise of the family.

African American women have it even harder. African women were brought to this country to work for no pay. Even with ratification of the 13th amendment in 1865, which put an end to slavery, it wasn't until 1868 that freed slaves were granted citizenship and protection under the law. As of mid-2014, only one of the women elected to the Senate was African American.[3] And the first African American CEO of a Fortune 500 company wasn't elected until 2009. As we discuss the evolution of women's rights in America, we must note that the African American woman's reality has been much different than the white woman's experience.

Sojourner Truth's speech in 1851 at a women's convention in Ohio, "Ain't I a woman?" called attention to the differences between the experiences of African American women; Truth spoke of no one holding doors for her or giving her the best of anything because she was a woman. Truth's speech inspired many activists for black feminism throughout history, including Zora Neale Huston, bell hooks (the pen name for Gloria Jean Watkins who chooses not to capitalize her name), and Rebecca Walker, among others. The evolution of women's rights has too often ignored the plight of black women.

History also shows that a woman who rebelled against domesticity and submission to her father or husband risked being committed to an insane asylum. In 1860, Elizabeth Packard was committed by her husband to an Illinois asylum because she disagreed with his Calvinist religious views.[4] He didn't want her to "ruin" the children with her heretical ways so he had her committed. At that time, all that was needed was a husband's testimony to commit his wife. After three long years, Packard was released from the asylum but her husband disappeared with her children and property, and she had no legal recourse whatsoever. Elizabeth Packard spent the rest of her life advocating for the rights of women and the mentally ill. She wrote numerous books and lobbied for more stringent commitment laws (requiring more than just a husband's word to commit his wife) as well as laws to give married women equal rights in matters of child custody and property.

In my own family tree, there is a branch with a woman who was declared insane soon after her husband's death. Her minor children were placed in guardianship of a male relative (her son-in-law), along with her property. It is impossible to tell by looking at the paperwork what was specifically wrong with this woman; however, it is easy to conjecture that my great-great-grandfather's death may have thrown his widow into a mental crisis of a contrived nature. If I were a woman in the 1800s whose husband died and left me without the right to my children or property, I may have acted in ways deemed "crazy" also. I am grateful that I did not live at that time—when dissatisfaction was treated as a medical malady rather than an impetus for change.

In literature, we find art blazing the trail on behalf of women's rights. Charlotte Perkins Gilman's *The Yellow Wallpaper* (written in 1892) shunned the popular medical practice of the "rest cure," calling into question the persona of the all-knowing, patriarchal figure of the male psychologist and the husbands who implemented the practice. The rest cure called for removal of all manner of passing one's time intellectually, such as reading or writing, so that concentration on "rest" could be achieved. The basic tenet was that women were feeble-minded and frail. It essentially kept them in captivity, cut them off from loved ones, and hurt rather than helped them. Charlotte Perkins was subjected to the rest cure during her first marriage (to Charles Stetson) to deal with depression after the birth of her daughter.

Another real-life example of a woman subjected to the rest cure was author Virginia Woolf, one of the major literary figures of the 20th century, who struggled with bouts of depression and nervous breakdowns throughout her adult years. According to biographer Julie Briggs, "Many of her breakdowns occurred after she finished writing a novel, and were probably made worse by treatments in which she was forced to rest and forbidden to work."[5] Virginia Woolf was sexually abused by two of her half-brothers when she was only six years old. Her mom died when Woolf was just 13; and her father and a sister died by the time she was 22. As many writers will attest, the process of writing can be therapeutic and a way of making sense of the world. It seems that each time Woolf's means of creative therapy ceased, she fell into a pool of life's misery. Although much of what has been written about Woolf has focused on her mental instability, Briggs offers the theory that Woolf's breakdowns were not evidence of insanity, but rather a sensitive person's quite sane response to the darkness and cruelties of life, including the horrors of World War II

(Woolf's husband was Jewish). In March 1941, at age 59, Woolf took her own life by filling her pockets with rocks and walking into the River Ouse; the current carried her away and she drowned.

As the 20th century dawned, women were not allowed to vote in the United States. This changed with the 19th amendment, ratified in 1920. Carrie Chapman Catt, a leading suffragette and founder of the League of Women Voters, told the story of when she was 13 years old and she asked why her mother was not going to town to vote like her father; "her sincere question was met with laughter and the reason that voting was too important a civic duty to leave to women."[6] Another poignant example of women being treated as second class citizens involved the placement of Alice Paul, leader of what became known as the National Women's Party, into solitary confinement in the mental ward of a prison in order to undermine her credibility with the public.

Later in the 20th century, Roe v. Wade (1973) brought about a huge change in women's lives with the legalization of abortion. A little-known bit of history on abortion is that up until the early 1800s, abortion before quickening (defined as first fetal movements) was *not* illegal, and only became illegal because surgical procedures during that period were highly risky due to the risk of infection (before the discovery of the antiseptic method for surgery).[7] The reason for enactment of anti-abortion laws was not to protect the fetus but to protect the life of the mother. It had nothing to do with the fetus' soul or religious views. Without delving into religious viewpoints about abortion, it is interesting to note that the Bible has passages that refer to the death of a fetus. One specifically deals with abortion in terms of loss of property and not sanctity of life; specifically differentiating between the loss of a man's wife from the loss of a fetus (e.g., if someone caused the loss of

26

a man's wife, this was punishable with "a life for a life," while cause of a miscarriage was punishable with a fine).[8] There are perhaps as many interpretations of the Bible as there are religions or Biblical scholars. I offer this information here as a point of historical detail.

From the early 1800s until the time of Roe v. Wade, women had little control over their reproductive organs. Indeed, this country saw a lot of "the unwilling bearing the unwanted."[9] At the time of this court decision, four-fifths of the United States enforced strict anti-abortion laws. It is no coincidence that this legislation was passed *after* women were given the right to vote. According to Susan B. Anthony, until women in America were given the right to vote, "the blessings of liberty (would be) forever withheld."[10] Her point was simple. Without female constituents, why would lawmakers care what they think?

Margaret Sanger was a nurse in the early 1900s who worked with poor women on the lower east side of New York and was well acquainted with the effects of unplanned and unwelcome pregnancies. Sanger's own mother suffered poor health after bearing eleven children (out of 18 pregnancies; dying at age 40). Sanger felt that women would not truly be free until they were in control of their reproductive rights.[11] Thus, Sanger came to view birth control—a term she is credited with inventing—as being integral to women's lives and health. In 1912, Sanger gave up nursing to dedicate herself to the distribution of birth control information. She was arrested under the Comstock Laws which made it illegal to send items considered obscene or lewd through the mail (the authorities declared that contraceptive information and devices were lewd). Sanger's many arrests and the resulting outcries helped lead to changes in laws, giving doctors the right to offer birth control information to patients. Sanger is the founder of Planned Parenthood Federation of America and said,

"Women must come to recognize that there is some function of womanhood other than being a child-bearing machine." Although Sanger died in 1966, her mission of protecting women's health, rights, and equality continues through Planned Parenthood's national and global efforts.[12]

The mid-20th century saw women firmly entrenched in the duties of the home—those of wife, mother, and homemaker. There were restrictions against pregnant women in the workplace; thus, pregnant women were not hired or were forced to relinquish employment once the pregnancy was discovered. As a "good wife and mother," women were expected to put their families ahead of their own wants and needs. Indeed, most had very few outlets for their attention outside the home.

During World War II, women went to work in factories when they were told by the U.S. government that it was their patriotic duty to fill the jobs vacated by the men who went to fight the war. The government even subsidized daycare to make it easier for mothers with young children. But when Johnny came marching home, the government withdrew all daycare subsidies and gave working women of the day their own marching orders. They were told that it was *now* their patriotic duty to vacate their jobs and get back into their homes, making way for the men who would be returning from the war and would want their jobs back.

My mother was one of these women—a 1950s housewife, with a domineering husband and five children, who had no voice or control over huge expanses of her life. Dr. Celia Halas wrote that women of my mother's generation felt powerless and inferior to their husbands because they were raised to defer to men; they were indoctrinated to believe that men were smarter and more capable which led to feelings of inadequacy and self-doubt. Even in moments where women felt they were right, their husbands blatantly

28

disregarded their opinions. The constant frustration of not being valued led to feelings of confusion and, eventually, a pattern of giving up or giving in. I can attest to this phenomenon in my home. Women of my mother's generation had little or no autonomy or decision-making authority in their own homes. Can you imagine being at home, day-after-day, for years on end (14 years in the case of my mom), without control over money, decision-making, or the ability to pursue anything other than domestic duties? Neither can I.

Betty Friedan published her book, *The Feminine Mystique*, in 1963, thereby putting a label on the feelings of restlessness women felt being confined to the home.[13] Friedan's book helped spark the second wave of the feminist movement (the first wave culminated with women's right to vote in 1920). The women's rights movement of the 1960s and 70s brought about a revolution in the workplace. In the 1960s, two-thirds of all new jobs went to women.[14] With the legalization of the birth control pill in 1960, the door was opened for women to pursue professional careers that required years of training uninterrupted by pregnancy, thereby fueling a wave of women who applied to medical, law, and business schools in the 1970s. The second wave of the feminist movement culminated with women commanding more diverse jobs, with higher pay, newfound self-reliance, and the ensuing steady shift in their roles at home. All this redefined what it meant to be female in America.

Having emerged from complete subordination to a more egalitarian partnership with men, women began earning their own money and were no longer reliant on men for financial security. Divorce rates skyrocketed and women became heads of households en masse. This evolution naturally changed the face of families. According to the U.S. Census Bureau, 45% of all households in America in

1960 were composed of married couples with children. That number dropped to 23% at the opening of the 21st century and has continued to drop.[15] During the 1990s alone, there was a 25% increase in the number of households headed by single mothers and a 71% increase in the number of households headed by unmarried partners.

As women have stepped out of the home into exciting, rewarding careers, isn't there a next logical step in women's social trajectory? A cessation of the idea that female success is inextricably tied to motherhood would be a step in the right direction.

We need to stop viewing the lives of females through the lens of motherhood. The fact is that no other life choice is as immediate or irreversible as becoming a mom. By being more upfront about what motherhood entails, with all its shades of reality, as well as encouraging other life choices, we can dispense with an outdated indoctrination program and take women's rights to a new level.

"I love people. I love my family, my children . . .
but inside myself is a place where I live all alone
and that's where you renew your springs that never dry up."
Pearl S. Buck, writer/humanitarian

Chapter 4: Dirty Little Secrets

There are things that our moms never tell us about their own experiences with motherhood. There are reasons they obscure the truth from our eyes. First, if they were to tell us just how hard it is, perhaps we might run away screaming and never make grandmothers of them. Indeed, it is a form of justice for moms to watch their own children become parents and experience that level of "I told you so" and recognition of the things moms actually go through. Another reason moms do not speak the truth about motherhood is that they love their kids and don't want to instill guilt in them for all the trials and tribulations that are par for the course. In accordance with the tenets of Motherhood Catechism, it is important to highlight the good stuff and minimize the not-so-good stuff. So we describe motherhood in all its glory. We swoon over our babies and marvel at their innocence as those "magical halos" materialize over their little heads every time they sleep. Never mind that it took three hours of walking the floor with a crying baby before she finally fell asleep.

Are there dirty little secrets that every mom keeps? Absolutely. Moms keep them tightly to their breasts so that they do not impede the evolution of humankind. But it's time to bring them to light.

Dirty Little Secret #1 – You will lose a big part of yourself once you become a mom. There are exceptions to this rule. If you are among the 1% of America who own 35% of all privately-held wealth (termed the "upper class"

31

by those who study wealth distribution in the U.S.[1]), then it is likely that you can afford a nanny, boarding school, or other means of helping you shoulder the responsibility of bringing up junior. This luxury can afford you the opportunity to live your life and keep your children too. For the remainder of moms, we will be at the beck and call of our children for the better part of our lives. The person you used to be is no more; she exists only to those who knew you B.C.—Before Children. All your energy is thrown into this endeavor called motherhood, and necessarily so. When your child wakes up with a fever on Mother's Day, don't call Hallmark. When your child starts puking in the middle of the night, you can welcome that 6 a.m. alarm clock with only two hours of sleep and bleary eyes.

I was 48 years old when I graduated with my bachelor's degree. My advanced age at attaining this goal is not completely the result of motherhood. I got married at the very tender age of 18, which was not uncommon in 1980. I'm of the baby boomer generation so female role models were largely housewives, teachers, nurses, and clerical workers. I followed in the footsteps of my mother and my two sisters by becoming a secretary. My decisions felt automatic, unquestioned. It didn't take me long to wish for more. But life marched on. Husband number one departed the scene and I left behind any ideas of returning to college. Several years later and in my second marriage, I yearned to finish my bachelor's degree. But husband number two did not have a biological child of his own, so we brought forth a child to our union, thereupon adding 18 more years to my "Motherhood Clock"—which is what I call the calculation of the years of exhaustive minute-to-minute, day-to-day, year-to-year responsibilities. After several starts and stops, I finally returned to school in earnest when my youngest was 7 years old. I'd been a mom for 20 years by that time. I spent the ensuing six years torn between job, husband, aging mother, children, and school, and not in that order. By the time I threw in some friends, siblings, and extended family members, I had so many hats to wear that I pretty much ignored my hat labeled "Self."

Dirty Little Secret #2 – Your "stuff" will never be your own again. Your scissors, tape, mascara, clothing—even spoons! Oh, and your toothbrush. Yes, it is all fair game and at some point will be touched, moved, or abused by your offspring.

Once upon a time, I had a silverware service for 12. That was B.C. My current supply of spoons has dwindled to less than half of the original number. I've interrogated my brood to no avail. The spoon mystery remains intact in our household. Then there was the day I found my toothbrush missing. Much to my horror, my teenage daughter had grabbed my toothbrush because she was *too lazy* to take 120 seconds to run upstairs and grab her own before dashing off to a dental appointment. This has a relatively high "ewww factor" as well as invading a basic tenet of personal space.

Other mothers tell stories of "the invasion." One mother told me how her tyke got hold of one of her diamond stud earrings and lost one, never again to re-surface. Another talked of a cherished bracelet her husband had given her B.C. and how years later, she was vacuuming up pieces of it after her child had broken it.

In her book, *Committed,* author Elizabeth Gilbert described how her grandmother Maude was born with a facial deformity; thus, it was assumed she would never marry and was encouraged to pursue an education and get a job—a nontraditional route for women during the Great Depression.[2] Maude worked and saved her money, dreaming of reconstructive surgery for her face. One day,

Maude splurged on a beautiful coat with a real fur collar. Gilbert's grandmother did get married—to a farmer—and Maude's savings was quickly absorbed into the farm. After the birth of her daughter, Maude cut up her cherished coat—the symbol of her youth and the most beautiful item she ever owned—and she made her baby girl an outfit. Gilbert describes her grandmother cutting up the finest and proudest parts of herself and giving it away. Clearly, people are more important than things, and this type of issue (people over things) comes up in everyday life with or without children. As a mother, let's just say that these occasions come up with unrelenting regularity.

Go on and tell yourself it'll be different for you. Or that you won't sweat the small stuff. With kids, it is the multitude of small stuff that slowly but surely sends you to the brink of your patience, where you teeter for years on end.

Dirty Little Secret #3 – Your sex life as you once knew it is on hold for about 18 years. Have another kid or two and that time period increases exponentially. No more loud outbursts in the bedroom. Spontaneous interludes are a thing of the past. Especially with teenagers in the house. A closed bedroom door in the middle of the day or early evening spells only one thing in their minds, even if one could possibly be as quiet as a mouse. Don't get me wrong, there are ways to make time for intimacy. But it takes forethought, creativity, and energy. And face it, creative energy is the one thing you don't have enough of with kids in the house. When the nest is once again empty, you find yourself older, with bodily functions that have a mind of their own, and with a lot less verve. This doesn't mean sex after children isn't enjoyable. It's just different. With forethought often doubling as foreplay.

Dirty Little Secret #4 – The length of time you spend not having control of your own schedule stretches over a great expanse of your lifetime. Basic freedoms that you took for granted B.C. become a thing of the past. For me, I've been a mom since I was 21 years old and I still have a high-schooler at home. Doing the math, I have not been able to go anywhere for 30 years of my life without first arranging some sort of childcare. I don't work, eat, or sleep without knowing the location of my offspring. And I certainly don't stray from the routine without considering how it will impact my child. There are no weekends away with my husband without the good graces of family or close friends who will watch my child. No spur of the moment jaunts. For years, this included the nightly walks that my husband and I relish. When our daughter was tiny, we could pop her into a stroller. But when she grew, kicking and screaming, out of her stroller, our walks together went on hiatus for about nine years until we felt comfortable leaving her at home for short periods of time. This may not sound like a lot to some people but for us, our nightly walk is what keeps us connected. It's when we have time to talk without interruption. We gave up over 1,000 evening walks in favor of our daughter over a nine year period. This is what we do for our children. They exert their control over our time and energy, and in return, we hope to watch them grow into fully-functional, well-adjusted, loving human beings.

At this writing, my daughter is 16 and I am watching my Motherhood Clock. I love and cherish her and will cry big, sentimental tears when she leaves the nest. While I cherish the now, I also look toward the future. When I embarked upon motherhood at age 21, I did not realize that it would take 31 years to see it through to the point where I would re-gain some of the spontaneity and control over my life. As I eye my Motherhood Clock, I am counting down the time until I can turn my focus to other endeavors…until I can travel without worrying about caregivers…and the day when all my belongings stay in the place I put them and don't grow little feet and scamper off.

Dirty Little Secret #5 – Kids need their moms way past the age of 18, or 22, or 30. Generation Y is very different than previous generations. The early 20s is now viewed by some psychologists as an extension of adolescence since it is common for young adults to remain in their parents' homes, somewhat dependent, and put off big life decisions until much later than previous generations. This is not completely the fault of generation Y-ers. The economy is drastically different and we're finding that young adults without a college education are greeted with a shorter list of opportunities after high school. During what economists call the Great Recession of 2008, my college graduate son lost his great first job. Through no fault of his own, he found himself unemployed and had to live with me much longer than either of us had anticipated. My other grown son has needed an enormous amount of support, including multiple failed trials with college, broken down cars, and a costly legal situation—all at my expense.

Even more than financial help is the physical and emotional help that kids still need way past their days of youth. The time I had a babysitter walk out on me in the morning before work, as a single mom who would have found the deduction of a day's pay devastating, who did I call? That's right. Crying into the phone, I called my mom. She responded by taking the day off from her own job so that she could save my day. That's how it is with moms.

My own phone has rung with various requests from my grown children. Including a particular call received at 3:00 in the morning that jolted me out of bed, expecting to hear the worst kind of news that typically only comes at that ungodly hour. It was my adult child. And I responded and listened. Yes, that's how it is with moms.

When it comes to setting limits, moms find that the line keeps moving. It is easy to speak of tough love, but when you find yourself in a circumstance where your child needs you, limits tend to move and stretch or fly completely out the window. It is easy to say what you think you would do, but until the situation presents itself, you cannot know. When a single female becomes pregnant and needs support, it is the rare mom who turns away. Whether it means giving up one's long-sought-after autonomy in the pre-retirement years, giving up one's physical space by taking daughter and grandchild into one's home, or becoming the back-up caregiver because of the lack of a father in the picture—whatever circumstances are associated with this situation, there are few limits on the assistance a mom is willing to give. This, too, is how it is with moms.

Dirty Little Secret #6 – This is probably the best kept secret of all. Mothers yearn for alone time. Married, single, it doesn't matter. This doesn't mean we want to be childless or spouseless or even friendless; far from it. It just means that after being "on call" for weeks that turn into months, and months that turn into years, and years that turn into decades, eventually we just want to spend a little time with ourselves to remember who we are. Or maybe we just want some time in the bathroom without someone talking to us through the door. Once upon a time, I was a person who only had to pack my own suitcase when I wanted to go somewhere. If I decided to drive 40 miles or 1,000 miles, I could do it without extensive preparations before pressing pedal to metal. After I became a mom, I learned that spontaneity was a whim of the past and even the smallest of adventures required ample amounts of planning.

There is a difference between a mom's need for alone time and a dad's. This difference centers on the traditional role that moms fill in orchestrating the vast details of childcare and family life. This is not intended to be a knock toward men; this is merely a statement of the reality in a majority of families. If you ask 100 women who takes responsibility in their homes for arranging babysitters, scheduling medical appointments, talking with children's teachers, going clothes shopping, and similar tasks, a greater percentage would answer that they do the majority compared with their children's fathers. So when talking about a mom's need for alone time, we are talking about a reprieve from the intensity of commitment—from the sometimes overwhelming sense of duty.

When Virginia Woolf wrote about having a room of one's own, she was referring to women needing time and space in order to reach literary achievement. In Woolf's day, there was a belief that women produced inferior works of literature. It was her contention that women were so absorbed with household duties that they didn't have time or a place in which they could hone their creative energy. Money seemed to be the primary element and effectual hindrance for women of that day since they did not have financial freedom. There is a line in Elizabeth Gilbert's book, *Eat Pray Love,* where she is sure that she no longer wants to be married. She writes, "I feel so overwhelmed with duty, tired of being the primary breadwinner and the housekeeper and the social coordinator and the dog walker and the wife and the soon-to-be mother, and—somewhere in my stolen moments—a writer..." It is easy to see why women in general, and specifically mothers, need time to themselves. They are, after all, separate entities with their own wants and needs apart from the needs of so many others. It is, however, often hard to discern the boundaries between women and their offspring.

One mother with two kids under age four jokingly referred to going to work as "the spa," because it represented a reprieve from the intensity that comes with the Pre-K ages. Another mother's excitement is palpable when she knows her husband is taking their four-year-old for an overnight at his parents' home a few hours away. While reading a book review, I came across a woman who expressed similar sentiments, "It took me almost five years to figure out that I need alone time. I need time away from my husband and my kids…in order *not* to feel like driving my car off a bridge just to check out. I need that time away to be the quality parent my children deserve."[3]

An example of the need for a room of one's own was with the writing of this book. The ideas had been bopping around in my head for so long, but I needed a time and a place to get my thoughts organized. After trying for months to write during stolen moments at home, I finally booked a hotel room for myself for a weekend so that I could have uninterrupted time in which to hone my creative energy. At the end of the weekend when I re-entered my home, my roles as mother and wife (etc.) pulled at my attention immediately. But the fact that you are reading this book is evidence of my victory. My house may not have been clean and my family may have felt somewhat ignored for bursts of time, but perseverance and fortitude eventually paid off.

So here's my own personal secret. Immediately after I finished my bachelor's degree in 2011, I began to set aside time to myself by taking occasional days off of work where I told not a soul of my plans. It took me 28 years of motherhood to reach the point where I started to try and fulfill my own needs in this arena; and the moments remained fairly rare. One summer, when my husband took a business trip to Italy and I got to go along, I secretly relished the arrangement that took us there on separate flights. I treasured the idea of spending 12+ hours completely on my own. I could revel in my own thoughts and nothing more. It was an "all about me" experience and I thoroughly enjoyed it. I love my husband dearly and we are wonderful travel companions. It's just that in my whole life, I can count the number of times I've traveled alone on one hand. To be alone is such a novel idea for me and I welcome the moments when they arrive.

Dirty Little Secret #7 – No discussion of dirty little secrets would be complete without four-letter words. No, I don't mean expletives. I'm referring to the words, um, "lice" (ugh) and "wait."

Lice, oh jeez, must we really talk about this one? Coming from an exceedingly reluctant expert on the topic, the answer is yes. When my two sons were young, we went through a cycle where they caught lice repeatedly through visits with people I had no control over. Something about my ex-husband's girlfriend and her kids, and her ex-husband's inability to eradicate the situation, and a family pet was involved; and well, it all came back to my home again and again. I became such an expert with the shampoo, nit-picking (nits are the lice eggs which multiply tenfold each day), spraying, vacuuming, endless loads of laundry, and tying up everything that couldn't be washed into airtight bags for 30 days. Needless to say, "Lice Removal Expert" is not one of those things I put on my resume. But expert I am. Which came in handy when my daughter caught lice as a youngster as well (apologies to my daughter: the nitty-gritty facts are being revealed). And when my 18-month old grandson had a brush with lice, who ya gonna call? That's right, call the Lice Expert!

The other four-letter word is "wait." Which means, parents must *wait* until their kids learn to sleep through the night, they must *wait* until they outgrow the biting or hitting stage, they must *wait* until their kids outgrow wetting the bed at night which can go on for years (apologies to my two sons, again, nothing but the facts)...parents must *wait* until their children learn the concept of sharing, they must *wait* until they learn a plethora of concepts that parents have drilled into their heads to the point of sounding like a tape-recording (pick up after yourself, remember to feed the cat, make sure you rinse your dishes before putting them in the dishwasher since everyone knows that dishwashers just get dishes *hot* and won't clean caked-on food; the list goes on and on). The concept of "wait" can be the hardest for parents to endure. But no worries! The present phase will eventually end! With another one around the corner that will push the qualms of the last one into the recesses of your mind.

Dirty Little Secret #8 – Kids are grounded in the belief that their moms revolve around them, even into adulthood. We've all done it. We've all asked way too much of our mothers. We've asked for babysitting services beyond what is reasonable. We've asked for financial assistance beyond what is comfortable. We look to our moms as our saviors and catch-alls.

For my children, I have funded failed college courses, paid expensive car repair bills, and shouldered a myriad of other extenuating requests. I'm not alone; as evidenced by my mother-in-law's "gift" to my husband on one of our first Christmases as a married couple. In a small box, she wrote a note, "I release you of all your debts to me." That note spoke volumes.

Parenting ideologies and theories abound. In the last few decades, we've gone from "A child should be seen and not heard," to the opposite extreme where children can be heard all over town (and all over the Internet). When children are brought up to believe that they are the center of their parent's universe, one must wonder how this translates into other relationships where empathy is a crucial life skill.

Now that we've shed some light on some of the best-kept secrets, if you still want to pursue motherhood, great! Just don't be surprised when most—or all—of these things become embedded into your life.

"I do not know how to express my thanks for all that you
have given me....For this, and for many other reasons,
I am proud to be your son.
I thank you above all else for believing in me.
When you believe in me, it becomes a reality."
Letter from a son to his mom

Chapter 5: Joys and Pains of Motherhood

There are definitely many amazing moments associated
with motherhood. Oh the joy of hearing phrases such as:
"Isn't my mom cool?!" and "You're cooler than my mom!"
The latter statement was actually uttered by...(gasp)...a
14-year-old friend of my daughter. Pretty powerful tonic to
say the least. Clearly, the quest to be cool is not what
motherhood is about. Some pursue this status a bit too
fervently and end up being more of a friend than a parent,
which can have detrimental effects on a child in desperate
need of responsible parenting. But in the course of being a
dutiful mom, the aforementioned comments were gratefully
received as validation of having done something right.

The celebrations of motherhood are varied. While writing
this chapter, Mother's Day occurred and my adult son
presented me with flowers and a card with the sweetest
handwritten note that brought tears to my eyes. My
children have the ability to buoy my spirits in magnificent
ways. Make no mistake: their happiness, health, and
safety are integral to my mental wellness. Whenever I pray
for anything, I preface each prayer with intercessions for
my children. Once a woman becomes a mother, she splits
herself into multiple parts, so to speak, and her life is never
the same. In the words of Elizabeth Stone, "To have a
child is to decide forever to have your heart go walking
around outside your body." Indeed, a mother's well-being
rests on these people who break off from her and the

ensuing years of ups, downs, successes, failures, and everything else that her offspring experience.

I've heard it said that the birth of a child is like the beginning of a love affair because it is a feeling of falling head over heels in love with this new little being that has entered your life. The amazement felt upon seeing the little person who grew for nine months inside your body is ineffable. Indeed, describing that moment is like Flaubert's cracked tin kettle—there does not seem to be the words to describe the emotions one feels when gazing at one's child for the first time.

This was not the case for one mother I interviewed, who said she didn't even want to hold her baby when he was born. Before casting judgment, know that this mother is the best kind of mother I've ever observed. She loves her son and is raising him to be a kind, considerate, loving human being. But she had plans for her life before she found out she was pregnant. That positive pregnancy test solicited the "oh shit" factor for her. The pressure of her upbringing and her family contributed to her decision to keep the baby. As I said, she's an amazing mom, she loves her son, and she does not regret her decision. She was just a bit underwhelmed at the beginning of her journey.

I remember the day I became a mom. Looking at my son's face, I felt a fierce protectiveness for my child and love coursed through my veins. These strong feelings felt by new moms are very lucky for the little people who keep them up nights for weeks and months and years on end; and put them through the rigors of life with children. It is that feeling of love and bonding that carries a mother through the ensuing challenges of the years to follow.

As my little son grew, the "love affair" continued. I rejoiced at his first smiles. My heart soared when he delivered his first kisses and hugs. All his "firsts" evoked great pride. It has been that way with all three of my kids. My children's accomplishments have felt like my own accomplishments. No matter how else I've messed up in my life, I have felt that if I can succeed in helping my children grow into loving, successful human beings, then I will have redeemed myself. It seems that some may carry this to an extreme; living vicariously through their children. Pushing them to make choices that they themselves wish they had pursued. Touting their child's accomplishments for the world to see as a way of saying, "See world, I did it right. I raised my child to do this! Hah! That must make me a really great person!" But what happens when the love story doesn't go as planned? Does that make a parent less of a great person?

The fact that the mother-child "love affair" does not always unfold like a fairy tale does not deter a woman from pursuing motherhood. Truly, sentimentality wins out over reality when it comes to the idea of becoming a mom. Moms are great. We love our moms. And so the script goes, "Who wouldn't want to be one?"

According to Dr. Celia Halas, author of *Why Can't a Woman Be More Like a Man?*, relationships are integral to females' lives. Marriage counselors have referred to women as relationship-barometers (a tidbit I learned long ago from a video on strengthening one's marriage). There's also evidence that one of the major factors that influence the statistic that women tend to outlive men relates to social connections. Psychologist Carol Gilligan conducted extensive research on females' concerns about abandonment/alienation, how they appear to others, and the importance of relationships. According to Gilligan, a female's "need to feel related to others is a crucial aspect of her identity."[1] It is understandable, therefore, that women find in motherhood what they seek in relationships:

45

a connection defined by unconditional love. We see the outstretched arms of our little ones and we feel that our place in this world is secure. We feel that we will always have these individuals who look up to us and love us. Obviously, these are good feelings. Whether the visions we have about our children actually pan out is a whole other story.

There are varying degrees of pain that come with motherhood. There's the emotional, stab-in-the heart pain, which can come about at a moment's notice. Perhaps your child is born with a disability and you wish you could take their struggles away, or an exchange of angry words between you and your child leaves a rift (especially poignant with adult children because the stakes are much higher).

Then there's the pain-in-the-ass pain such as when your four-year-old downs two cans of pop at a party when you're not looking and then proceeds to sit down on your lap and upchuck all over you. There you are, standing in a hot mess, ready to join your child in losing your lunch. You're at someone else's home, so what is there to do? You climb into your car, thankful for vinyl seats that can be scrubbed down later, roll down your windows and floor the accelerator until you are back across town and can run into the house and rip your disgusting clothes from your body, choking for fresh air.

Then there's physical pain, such as…childbirth. Any woman who has breastfed a newborn can attest to the pain in the first week or so when her nipples go through the roughening-up process, grimacing through those first 10 to 15 seconds of baby's insistent suckling until the pain-deadening hormones kick in as the milk rushes forth. Or how about a whack on the nose by a toy drumstick that someone thought was a great idea to buy your one-year-old? Ah yes, that's the ticket.

As our children grow, we roll with the punches, so to speak. Like the punch in the stomach when you find out that your eight-year-old son has been made fun of at school because of an inept teacher who does not know how to deal with a highly-active child with attention span challenges. Thanks to some insensitive remarks by one teacher, an entire class has learned to make fun of your child. And since you are too busy as a single mother, working full-time and keeping up with the routines of life, you haven't had the downtime necessary to talk with your child until the teasing has gone on for weeks. Then there's the proverbial punch in the gut when your 13-year-old daughter has her first crush and you realize there's been…kissing. Or the first time your child screams, "I hate you," when in fact, the impetus for the outburst is because you are trying your damnedest to be a responsible parent who pays attention.

A child truly holds his mother's heart in his hands. If your child goes missing for five minutes in the mall or your teenager is an hour past curfew, your heart skips a beat as you struggle for breath and your mind races from one dangerous scenario to the next. When your child is in pain, there is a feeling of sheer helplessness. God forbid the worst happens and you find yourself a childless mother. Parents live in fear of this kind of pain. I have a friend who lost her son when he was four. He was born with a handicap that contributed to his death, and she held him in her arms while he died. I think it was then that I began praying to God and the universe not to ever think that I have the strength to endure that kind of emotional pain. My mom lost her son (my brother) to a sudden heart attack at age 50. This man exercised daily, never smoked, and gave up his motorcycle in the days when he worked in a hospital emergency room, seeing person after person succumb to someone else's stupidity. Six months after my mom lost her son, her heart grew weak and she had to have a pacemaker implanted. My view is that the experience of losing her son literally broke her heart.

The fact that a piece of you is out there in this big, scary, indifferent world really doesn't hit you until your child starts becoming independent. It happens slowly and then increases in velocity with adolescence—that gradual letting go that starts sooner than expected and continues throughout a lifetime. One day, you find your child is speeding across the U.S. in a rented moving van with his new spouse by his side and you are offering up prayers for their safety. Or maybe your child signs up for the military and you know that she will be in harm's way and there's nothing that you can do about it. Or perhaps a recession has caused your child to lose his job and you watch helplessly as he grows more and more depressed until one day you find him sitting on the edge of his bed, wearing his winter coat, staring into space and talking about how he tried to find an open church so he could go and pray; and your child's desperation resonates in your very soul. Emotional pain of the most acute kind is what you feel when you are scared for your child. For this kind of pain, age is of no consequence. Fourteen or 40, we feel our child's pain with the sharpest of emotions.

A friend said to me a long time ago, "Motherhood is bittersweet." I did not understand those words until I became a mother myself. For me, bittersweet has been the taste of my birthday that comes and goes without my grown child attempting to reach me. Or the teenager who lashes out with words of contempt. We rejoice when children utter their first words and then later, we are injured by that same power of speech. We teach them independence and then we are filled with sadness when they are too busy to call us. Bittersweet is when, despite our best efforts, our kids fall short of the basic expectations we had for them as they were growing up. Expectations that they'll become responsible, self-sufficient individuals, caring, good citizens, and that they'll call us on our birthdays.

As a seasoned parent with adult children, I realize that moments like these are to be expected. But when I started out on this adventure called motherhood, I had expectations for myself as a "good mother" who would produce the "good child" who would never intentionally inflict pain toward me.

This is part of the reality of motherhood that remains cloaked in silence. We are told that motherhood is fulfilling, rewarding, and will round out our lives. We are told to expect the fairy tale and the happily-ever-after. There are rewards to motherhood; but there are equally as many sacrifices and frustrations. The fact is, once you choose motherhood, life as you know it ceases to exist; and by default, you must forego many other choices that could be equally as rewarding. Weighing the options for one's life should take place within a setting of knowledge, openness, and acceptance.

"We don't see things as they are,
We see them as we are."
Anaïs Nin, author

Chapter 6: Secret Sorority

"I didn't know when you had a baby you crossed a river into another country, a country of mothers. Now I feel an instant connection to any other woman with a child. We *know*. It's like a secret society. And I finally belong." This is how writer Virginia Woodruff described her experience of becoming a mom.[1]

I sat down with Najina,* a petite woman in her mid-30s who has chosen not to have children. At a family-owned coffee shop, we talked at length about motherhood, the pressures women are under to pursue it, and what it's like for her to live with her choice of being childless in our society.

Najina said, "It's as if there's a secret community and I'm never going to be a part of that." Even though Najina is completely happy with her life and her choice to never have children, she lives in a culture that often casts her difference from her peers who are mothers in a negative light. On the whole, American culture treats motherhood like a sorority where you are made to feel "less than" if you're not a member of the club. Najina regularly hears comments such as, "Oh, you just don't know what tired is." These comments have the effect of minimizing Najina's own experiences.

If, on the other hand, Najina were to carry on about how much she enjoys waking up late on a weekend morning,

---

* Names have been changed

spending all day reading a book if she wishes, or walking into the travel section of a bookstore, closing her eyes, and pointing to the next destination that she and her significant other will embark upon, these same mothers might be treated to a view of the flip side of the motherhood coin; the community of females who are not mothers who really do enjoy life without children. Najina lives a life filled with meaning and happiness—*her* version of meaning. A teacher and a person of captivating warmth, Najina choked up when discussing her class, "If my students leave my classroom feeling positive…that they've grown because of something I've taught them, I feel so good."

Najina is an aunt, a daughter, a friend, and a significant other to a man who shares her views on foregoing parenthood. It hadn't occurred to Najina that opting out of motherhood was a viable life choice until she encountered a female teacher in college who did not have children of her own, and this woman became a mentor. It was only then that she started envisioning a life without motherhood. What if Najina had not met this particular teacher? Would she have continued to live her life fulfilling the expectations she internalized while growing up? Can we imagine how many other "Najinas" are not encouraged to pursue their own versions of a meaningful life?

Ethnocentrism is the belief that the ways of a group or culture are superior to those of other groups. The ethnocentric person believes that people who do not exhibit what they define as "correct" behaviors are strange or dysfunctional. This term can be applied to the culture of motherhood. When women are told what lives they should want for themselves, it is understandable that they would feel that they don't fit in unless they conform to the ideals of those around them.

At the opposite end of the spectrum from ethnocentrism is cultural pluralism—a condition in which minority groups feel accepted in the dominant society and live their lives without criticism and external pressure to assimilate. What might cultural pluralism look like with regard to motherhood? With the minority of the female population being those who end their childbearing years never having borne a child of their own (approximately 20%),[2] we might see those women living lives free from judgment, cajoling, or pity. It might mean that a female's inclination *not* to become a mother would be encouraged by those around her, making it easier to choose a life in pursuit of the goals that feel authentic to her. It would mean that women without children would not feel like outcasts; nor would they feel the need to explain their reasons for not having their own children.

Viktor Frankl, a psychologist and survivor of the Nazi concentration camp in Auschwitz, wrote in his book, *Man's Search for Meaning*, that in a place where survival hung in the balance on a minute-to-minute basis, finding meaning in one's life meant the difference between life and death.[3] Frankl described how a prisoner wasted away in two days after he gave up his belief that the future held meaning for him. Frankl goes on to discuss his theory of "logotherapy" (logos is the Greek word for meaning), which teaches that there are "three main avenues on which one arrives at meaning in life...by creating a work or doing a deed, by experiencing something or encountering someone...(or by) turning a personal tragedy into a triumph."

Finding meaning in one's life is an individualized endeavor; yet females continue to hear the same messages that their mothers and grandmothers heard—messages that *sound* different but remain the same. The 21st century female is encouraged to pursue education and career, while retaining the familial duties of motherhood and domesticity. There are countless magazines chock full of advice on how women can cook faster, deal with cleaning more efficiently, and similar topics designed to help them do more in less time! But not every woman finds that these endeavors fit into their idea of a meaningful life.

Women who are not mothers speak of tedium at being constantly exposed to images that tout the world they are not a part of. Media plays a huge role in this. As do their friends. We can all be guilty of obsessing about various aspects of our lives, without realization of the tiresome effect on those around us.

Myself, I happen to be a gardener, and I love to watch the evolution of my little Eden from spring through fall. But if I insisted upon crooning about how I finally got hollyhocks to grow after years of defeat or my chagrin at the incessant nibbling down of my blossoms by the denizens of the outdoor world (ravenous rabbits!), would it be presumptuous of me to assume that everyone within earshot would be interested in my stories?

Author Delia Ephron made this point in her book, *Sister Mother Husband Dog: Etc.*, a compilation of essays in memoir fashion, and one of the chapters is all about her dog.[4] How she found her dog, her previous dog, her dog's personality, medical afflictions, etc. She prefaced the chapter with a disclaimer that for those without pets, or those who have never known the love of a pet, that perhaps they'd like to skip the chapter. At the chapter's conclusion, she quips, "Now you can tell me all about your grandchildren." Point taken.

A graphic designer from Washington state, Emma* describes how the majority of her friends are wrapped up in

---

* Name has been changed

their lives with children. Emma says, "I feel alone and not part of the club." When her friends call to talk about their pregnancies, Emma fakes excitement. It means one less friend who will have time for her. Emma grew up assuming she would have kids someday, "Everyone around me had kids, it's just what people did." Having met her husband in her late 30s, Emma and her husband do not find parenthood appealing. Except that they live in an area with many young families, so the topic is constantly in-their-face, so to speak. Emma longs for more like-minded friends where she and her husband would fit in.

A soft-spoken 27-year-old junior high school teacher, Calista[*] does not want children of her own. When co-workers have learned of her choice, she has felt "almost embarrassed" because of their bewildered reactions. Calista regularly hears, "If you don't want to have a child, then *why* are you a teacher?" Calista always knew she wanted to be a teacher; when she got her own classroom it was the fulfillment of her dream. She knows she is doing what she is meant to do. She just wishes her disinterest in becoming a mother would be widely accepted as "normal."

Calista's situation is not uncommon for teachers. The media joins in treating childless women as though they do not fit in with their cohorts who are parents. In an article entitled, "Parents Make Better Teachers," Sara Mosle stated that when she first became a teacher, she was "single, childless, and clueless about even the most basic aspects of child-rearing."[5] Two decades later, she returned to teaching, this time as a mother, "I was acutely aware of how being a parent made me a better teacher." Although feelings such as Mosle's are subjective, unfortunately, articles that demean the skills of childless women feed the bias that these women are somehow inferior to those who *are* mothers.

Teachers are not the only ones who find that their careers get mixed up with their status as nonmothers. Cathy* has a medical practice and related how a past business partner asked her, "What's your problem?" because she was in her 30s and had no children. It seems her status as a nonmom somehow made their company seem less "family-friendly." Cathy's story is similar to that of another single woman who ran for mayor and was reportedly described by her opponent, a man with a wife and kids, as not exhibiting sufficient family values since she had no kids of her own. Enough people disagreed and the childless female challenger won the mayoral race!

In Hispanic culture, getting married and having kids is "just what you do," according to Selena,* who receives constant questions from both family and friends. "Most of the questions come from other women...they're so concerned that I'm lonely or unhappy...I've been told to 'Snap out of it!'" Selena is in her mid-20s and describes herself as "not a kid person." She realizes that she is in the minority among her family and friends and that some pity her. One family member brings up the topic frequently. Even though Selena understands that it is out of concern—that others want her to be a part of the club (read: happy, not lonely)—Selena doesn't like that the topic comes up so often.

An HR professional in her 60s, Leala's* goal once was to become a mother. Now divorced, she described how her marriage fell apart due in large part to her husband's insistence upon cloaking his sterility with secrecy once it was discovered that it was due to a childhood disease. His attempt to protect his parents from possible feelings of guilt left Leala a prime target for derogatory comments from his family since they thought she chose her career over having

---

* Names have been changed.

55

a family. Leala did not measure up in their eyes. Being shunned and made to feel "less than" by her husband's relatives eventually took its toll; Leala didn't want to live that way anymore.

When women are indoctrinated to believe that they should pursue it all, including motherhood, it means that those women who are never able to physically bear children for medical reasons are left feeling like they have an empty hole in their lives that they can never fill. For those who marry men who don't wish to have children, they may feel pressure to change their husband's mind. Or for those who approach the end of their fertility without having found a partner or the right situation in which to raise a child—and are not interested in solo-motherhood—these women are faced with the decision of whether to freeze their eggs (thanks to advances in reproductive technology) or try to make peace with their life situation.

The women who suffer the most because of their indoctrination into Motherhood Catechism are those who are not able to have children due to a medical or fertility problem, but want very much to become members of the club. Madelyn Cain's book, *The Childless Revolution*,[6] contains poignant interviews with women who were plagued with anguish and depression when faced with childlessness under these circumstances. They wanted motherhood, they expected it, and many endured multiple trials of painful and expensive fertility treatments to achieve it; with devastating results. One such interview is haunting: Donna said, "I thought, if I can't have children, there's no reason to live." While researching this book, I found a version of Cain's Donna; someone I've known a very long time but never realized the depth of her pain. This woman struggled with infertility and remembers feeling, "If I can't have children, what's life about?"

56

Does any one of us want this kind of misery to envelope a female in our lives? Is it possible that a woman dealing with the loss of her dream of motherhood could have her feelings ameliorated if society did *not* promote motherhood so avidly? There are many women who are pushed to the brink of despair, and they are surrounded by images that reflect the life they *assumed* they would lead but cannot achieve. We simply *must* acknowledge a correlation between the assumptions held for their lives and the intensity of pain that women, such as Cain's Donna, feel when they are unable to fulfill their goal—a goal that they were indoctrinated to believe is the essential ingredient that makes life worth living.

Olivia* is deeply religious but she no longer attends church on Mother's Day. Olivia grew up with the assumption that she'd be a mother someday, but the experience did not happen for her. On Mother's Day, the ritual of having all mothers stand for a special blessing is painful for Olivia. People who take part, including pastors and the congregation, do not intend for anyone to feel left out. But that's the reality for many women in Olivia's situation. In truth, many childless women stop practicing their religion (or switch religions) because they feel excluded.

Psychologist Abraham Maslow's infamous theory on human motivation, "The Hierarchy of Needs," is a five-stage model that explains how one's most basic needs must be satisfied before one is motivated to try to meet the next level of needs.[7] The concept is that satisfaction of each tier takes place in sequential order; the most basic needs must be met before one can move on to the next set of needs. The first tier is physiological in nature (food, shelter, sleep), and the second tier refers to safety needs (security of employment and resources, law and order). Maslow's third

---

* Name has been changed

57

tier of basic human needs is social in nature, "Belonging," defined as love, connection, and feeling a part of something.

According to Dr. Ruth A. Wilson, the basic need of belonging receives far less attention than it should.[8] She writes, "The results of not having belonging-needs met are usually serious…belonging happens only within a social context. Social groups that support a sense of belonging operate in an inclusive way; an inclusive environment reflects the understanding that we're all the same yet different. That is, we all have certain needs, rights, and desires in common, but we're also unique individuals. Establishing an environment that honors both a shared identity and the individual identities of members within a group is a challenge that can be met only through the cooperation of people within the group." Is it possible to envision a sisterhood where all females support each other out of recognition that they are all a part of the larger group?

I once heard a comment about Oprah Winfrey that epitomizes the viewpoint that every person must procreate or all they do in their lifetime is for naught. Despite all that Oprah Winfrey has achieved, some people feel that all her successes are for nothing because she has no one to leave her legacy to since she has no children of her own. How does one explain this comment about a woman who has helped establish 60 schools in 13 countries, has supported women's shelters, built youth centers and homes, and changed the future for people all over the world?[9] Some-one to leave her legacy to? Oprah's legacy has a life of its own; and consists of every life she's touched.

As the first African American woman to anchor the Nashville news in 1973, Oprah has inspired thousands, if not millions, of young women of many ethnicities. She is not a woman who dislikes children. Indeed, her commitment to children led her to testify before the U.S. Senate Judiciary Committee to establish a national database of convicted child abusers; a part of the National Child Protection Act which was signed into law in 1993 by President Clinton; referred to as the "Oprah Bill." When asked why she chose not to have her own children, Oprah simply replied, "I never felt compelled to do it."[10] No matter her achievements, some regard her as lacking because she is not a mother.

For me, and for so many other American females, becoming a mother felt more like a foregone conclusion than a conscious choice. Oh we may have told ourselves it was our choice. But was the choice ever *if* or was it really *when*? Even for those couples who seriously discuss never having children, is the option not to have at least one child ever really there? Some will answer yes, but I'm not so sure. To say "no" to having your own family feels as though you are shunning the family values system that is so ingrained in society. The pressure is intense and, for many, impossible to ignore.

In my own experience, after having gone through a divorce with two young children and becoming a single mom, I got re-married to a man who did not have a biological child of his own. The scene at my bridal shower included the whole ribbon breaking routine, and that's when my future mother-in-law made a seemingly innocent statement that we "had to have at least one child." At that time, I had two young sons from my first marriage and my energy was taxed to the breaking point due to a full-time job, the demands of motherhood, and a myriad of other responsibilities. I felt that I did not have it in me to mother another child in the way that I thought that child deserved. A few years into our marriage, my mother-in-law's statement weighed on my mind. There was a part of me that felt I was letting someone down. Who that someone was, I wasn't quite sure.

Those feelings were exacerbated by people who would ask us *when* we were ever going to have a kid. This type of questioning took place at multiple family functions; once in a loud, somewhat rude manner of inquiry that communicated volumes. It was as if we were committing a sin not to have gotten down to the business of procreation. I was offended by the thought that our personal decision was being judged as "wrong." I resented this line of thinking then and I still do. For the record, my husband and I did have our own child (my third child); a daughter whom I love and adore. The decision to have a third child revolved around my love for my husband and a desire to see him experience biological fatherhood. Contributing to this decision was my ability to reduce my work schedule from full-time to part-time, allowing me the chance to reallocate energy to a third child. However, I would be lying if I didn't admit that the expectations of others entered into my decision of having another child.

We like to believe that we are masters of our own destinies. But is this fact or illusion? Do the expectations of our families, friends, religious leaders, and society-at-large weigh heavily on our minds and predetermine our choices? Who among us is brave enough to throw off the chains wrought of others' expectations? Oprah Winfrey is just one example of a woman who has done this. But in Oprah's case, it is easier for her to justify her choice because she has done so much for so many. What about those women who are everyday people with everyday lives? They're not out there building schools and women's shelters. But don't they deserve to live authentic lives also?

Living an authentic life is easier when all females are celebrated, no matter their life experiences.

Page intentionally left blank

Part II

Reality Check

"When a man gives his opinion, he's a man. When a
woman gives her opinion, she's a bitch."
Bette Davis, actor

Chapter 7: Double Standards

If a man opts to remain a bachelor and childless, he is
labeled a playboy. If he toils long hours at work in order to
climb the corporate ladder, he is deemed serious about his
career and a dedicated breadwinner. However, if a woman
opts *not* to become a mother, society labels her selfish,
damaged or dysfunctional. She is pitied and people wonder
what went wrong in her life that left her childless.
Twenty-five years ago, my former co-workers shook their
heads in disbelief upon discussion of an older, single,
childless, very successful business woman in our
workplace. She was almost 40 at the time and had worked
her way up to a top management position in a male-
dominated corporate environment. If she were a man, no
one would have thought twice about it. But the water-
cooler talk of the day was that of consternation. She may
as well have affixed a scarlet letter to her bosom so that all
could join in the judgment of her ignominious lifestyle.

Two books published in 2014 advised women how to
navigate the playing field of career, marriage, and babies.
These two books appear to be at opposite ends of the
spectrum, but espouse a similar message. In *Marry Smart,*
Susan Patton advises women to snag a husband during
college because if they focus on their careers first and look
for a husband later, they'll have to compete with women
who are younger, fresher, and "dewy-eyed."[1] Patton says,
"Work will wait. Your fertility won't." In *Lean in For
Graduates,* Sheryl Sandberg advises women to lean into
their careers from the starting gate (after graduation) so that
they can work their way up the career ladder as quickly as

possible, allowing them to "lean out" when the time comes to have children.[2] While Patton's book rewinds the rhetoric on women's lives by decades, Sandberg's book, with its feminist leanings, still espouses procreation as the driving force behind women's actions. Conversely, the library aisle with books advising men on this topic is…empty.

Clearly, women are held to different standards than men when it comes to career aspirations and family values. Why is it that a man can opt out of fatherhood without fear of reproach from his friends but a woman feels the full impact of her choices through the lenses of all those around her?

When author Maeve Binchy passed away in 2012, as a part of her obituary, reporter Amanda Craig of *The Telegraph* wrote, "Binchy would have been a better writer had she been a mother, giving her a deeper understanding of human nature."[3] Maeve Binchy was an Irish novelist, playwright, short story writer, and columnist, known for her descriptive characters and her interest in human nature. Her bestselling novels were translated into 37 languages and sold more than 40 million copies worldwide. One must ask, has any male author who created a father character in a novel ever been criticized for not having been a father himself? The narrow-mindedness of this particular double standard is hard to fathom.

Literature is full of examples of women who wanted something else for their lives and were judged harshly for trying to do so. In Kate Chopin's *The Awakening*, the main character is Edna Pontellier, a wife and mother in the late 1800s. Edna lived her life in accordance with society's expectations; however, she yearned for something different. Up to that point, she'd been going through the motions of life, going with the flow, doing what others expected her to do. She had married, had children, and was living a life of servitude to the whims of her husband and children. She described her attachment to her children with fondness, but not the kind of intense love that society associates with "maternal instinct." Something inside Edna awakens to the idea that just because she's a woman, she doesn't have to do everything society tells her she should. She begins to uncover parts of herself she'd kept buried her whole life.

A contemporary version of *The Awakening* is Elizabeth Gilbert's *Eat Pray Love*. Gilbert also finds herself caught in the midst of someone else's "dream life" and awakens in time to escape a marriage where she was going through the motions; a marriage in which children were very much a part of the plan, even though she felt no maternal desire to have them. In the vein of internalizing society's judgment of women who do not stick to the program, Gilbert refers to herself as a "criminal jerk" and falls into a deep depression, fully believing that there's something wrong with her for not wanting what she's "supposed" to want.

The arm of culture is long and strong and reaches into all our lives, coloring our actions, choices, and self-perception. The ideal of procreation and having one's own nuclear family is strongly dictated in America. But it is important to keep in mind that strong family values can take many different forms. My brother, who died at age 50, never had any children of his own but he had some of the strongest family values of anyone I've known. He loved to travel home for holidays and catch up with his family. My brother did not live any less a full life because he opted out of the title of Dad. He had decided that if he didn't find the right conditions to embark upon fatherhood, then it was not for him. My brother wanted to approach parenthood under the circumstances he felt best for any child of his or not at all. It is easier for a man to stand by this kind of decision than it is for a woman. After all, men don't have the pressure of the biological clock that women have. As women's "good eggs" begin to dwindle, a man holds onto his virility into his twilight years. As evidenced by actor Tony Randall who fathered his first child at age 77 (and a second child at 79).

Vickie* is 42, has her MBA, a senior management position, and she has no children (yet). Vickie and her husband have been married three years and were undergoing their second round of in vitro fertilization when we spoke. Vickie lamented, "I just wish my biological clock was longer; I wanted to be married longer before having a baby...there are still things I want to do."

There is also a double standard pertaining to the quality of life enjoyed by a father versus a mother. Charlotte Perkins Gilman, a writer and 19th century feminist who crusaded tirelessly for women's rights, wrote, "We have so arranged life that a man may have a home, a family, love...father-hood, yet remain an active citizen of age and country. We have so arranged life, on the other hand, that a woman must 'choose'; must either live alone...childless, with her work in the world for sole consolation; or give up all world service for the joys of love, motherhood, and domestic service." Gilman makes a point that was true in the 19th century and is true today. Men can have it all with regard to work and family. While women who try to have it all end up exhausted and pulled in too many directions.

Achieving work-life balance is a hot topic for today's mothers working outside the home who juggle the demands of everyday life, employment, and children's needs—sometimes with a spouse to help—but increasingly, women are left with a solo juggling act. The popular term used to describe moms who do not work outside the home is "Stay-at-Home Mom." These moms also find work-life balance a

---

* Name has been changed

sticky topic. They can attest to the seemingly endless, 24/7 to-do list that keeps them from attending to their own needs, while their partners come and go with greater ease.

In homes with a father present, it is the minority of dads who actively and fully participate in the orchestration of family life. According to a 2011 study by the Center for Work & Family at Boston College, 963 fathers working in white-collar jobs were surveyed, and 70% said that they strived to share parenting responsibilities equally with their spouses but failed to do so.[4]

The face of fatherhood in America is slowly changing. The number of dads who forego paychecks to care for their kids has risen from 1.6% of all "Stay-at-Home" parents in 2001 to 3.4% in 2011.[5] These numbers are minuscule and not at all surprising to me personally. With almost three decades of parenting experience, and 25 of those years spent working alongside other mothers in the workplace, I have heard possibly thousands of comments about the lack of balance between what mothers and fathers do around the home. Indeed, this lack of balance is often fodder for jokes. I did an informal poll of mothers in my immediate sphere—all were moms working outside the home—and the result was 100% that they and their child's father do *not* have a 50/50 balance with regard to the load of childcare and household tasks.

Don't get me wrong, there are some highly participatory dads out there, but they are the minority. Of the ones who are not highly participatory, many are good dads and they love their kids; they work hard to support them and they have good intentions. Clearly, there's a lot of room for improvement in the double standard area of work-life balance.

When scanning the magazine aisles, one finds magazine titles such as *Working Mother, Parents, Family Circle, Good Housekeeping, Better Homes and Gardens,* along with a plethora of other magazines touting articles on how to be an unflappable mom, how to cook nutritious meals in 20 minutes flat, make easy crafts on rainy days, and other articles that appeal to a mother's yearn for balance in her life. (Pssst: Where is the *Working Father* magazine?)

According to a report issued by the U.S. General Accounting Office (GAO) in October 2003, "Men with children appear to get an earnings boost, whereas women lose earnings. Men with children earn about 2% more on average than men without children...whereas women with children earn about 2.5% less than women without children."[6] This double standard in pay equity appears significantly tied to the differences in men's and women's work patterns according to the GAO, including more leave from work to care for family which tends to suppress women's wages.

Dating back to 1963, the year that the Equal Pay Act was signed into law, women earned 58.9% of the wages men earned (59 cents to men's dollar). Forty-nine years later, in 2012, women earned 76.5% compared to men's earnings (about 77 cents to men's dollar).[7] That is a narrowing of the wage gap by 17.6%—less than half-a-cent per year.

In addition, the glass ceiling appears to be a little higher but, by and large, still firmly in place. The GAO reports that in 2007, an analysis of 13 industries showed that "women were less than proportionately represented in management positions than in non-management positions."[8] The report indicates that a good amount of the differences in wages and mobility can be attributed to motherhood; from hiring practices, to the value placed on females in the workplace, to time taken off from work either short-term or extended.

What all these double standards mean is that females should weigh their options carefully. Basing their decisions on the experiences of their mothers and grandmothers is no longer prudent. Motherhood is a whole new ballgame. For society to continue to tout motherhood as the idyllic picture of the "fulfilled woman" misses the mark, and misrepresents the new reality of the female experience.

"There are all kinds of Mothers…to think you understand who a woman is because she's a Mother is a mistake."
Phylicia Rashad, actor/singer

Chapter 8: The Faces of Motherhood

While we may have idyllic images of what motherhood can be, with cherubic children calmly and happily riding in the back of the minivan as you drive off for a family vacation, the reality is often very different. Katrina Alcorn wrote a book called *Maxed Out* about being an American mom trying to balance the demands of work and family.[1] She wrote, "Years of unceasing activity—and the attendant stress and exhaustion—have a way of catching up with us." Alcorn started experiencing panic attacks, insomnia, and depression. She quit her job and underwent therapy; it was a year before she worked again.

Alcorn cited a survey where 88% of mothers (nearly 500 respondents) said they suffered stress-related health issues since having kids and going to work outside the home. Women described depression, anxiety, even seizures. Alcorn speaks of systemic measures for parents to meet their competing obligations; without which, we have the makings of a public-health crisis. Alcorn is one of the more fortunate moms who had a safety net (financially) when her health imploded; mothers in lower-income categories may lose their homes or worse when faced with similar circumstances.

In a 2010 report by the Center for American Progress (CAP), work-life conflict among families was broken down into "Three Faces," according to income level.[2] With the exception of the wealthiest Americans, the three faces are comprised of: "The Poor/Low-Income" (the bottom one-third with an annual median salary of $19,000); "The

Professionals" (the top 20% with an annual median salary of $148,000—with one in five earning above $210,000); and "The Missing Middle" (50% of American families earning an annual median income of $64,000).

With government programs geared toward low-income families, and the top 20% earning well above the majority of other Americans, the CAP report stresses that it is middle-income families that "get lost in the shuffle between the professional mothers praised for staying at home and poor mothers criticized for doing so." Referring to "The Missing Middle," Harvard sociology professor Theda Skocpol is puzzled because "policy debates deal so little with the fate of working families of modest means, the people who put in long hours to earn a living…coping with rising pressures in their workplaces while trying to raise children in solo-parent or dual-worker families."

The CAP report documents a growing income divide from 1979 to 2008. Adjusted for inflation, low-income families' earnings plummeted 28.8% over three decades; middle-income families' earnings plummeted 13.2%; and professionals' earnings rose 7.4%. The reasons for the divergence of incomes are varied. The U.S. has experienced dramatic changes in the economy. Manufacturing and agriculture jobs have dwindled; in their place are specialized service jobs (technology, healthcare, education, etc.) as well as lower-paid service jobs (hospitality, retail, etc.).[3] Whereas hard work and a high school diploma used to pave the way to a piece of the American dream, this has become increasingly harder to achieve. At the same time, the price tag of a college degree has skyrocketed.

In addition, CAP reports, "The typical American workplace is so deeply out of sync with today's workforce because of dramatic changes over the past few decades to incomes, working hours, and patterns of family care…Today's model is still in line with the workforce of 1960 when only 20% of mothers worked outside the home, and the male breadwinner was expected to be available for work anytime, anywhere, for as long as the employer needed him." With 70% of American children living in households where all adults are employed, today's workplace model no longer works for the majority of families.

According to an analysis by the Organization for Economic Cooperation and Development, out of 38 countries (from Austria to Estonia to Iceland, Korea, Mexico and Turkey) the United States is the only country out of 38 that does *not* have a paid maternity leave policy.[4] The only legislation passed in support of families in the past two decades is the Family and Medical Leave Act (passed in 1993), which is unpaid and covers about half the labor force.[5]

CAP describes the work-family conflict for a typical low-income family: they often have jobs with unstable schedules that require mandatory overtime, with rigid "no-fault" systems (attendance points docked for arriving at work a few minutes late), lack of sick pay or paid family medical leave, and they work multiple jobs to make ends meet.[6] They cannot afford quality daycare and depend on extended family members or older siblings to watch younger siblings—or the children are left home alone.

What do the above statistics tell us about the faces of motherhood in America? According to where you fall within the three income categories, your motherhood experience will be vastly different.

Working outside the home has never been a true choice for many mothers. Well-meaning books that talk about the "on and off-ramps" of motherhood do not resonate with those who have no choice. These books are aimed at women who are able to take the "off-ramp" from their careers, either by staying at home for a period of time or cutting their schedules to part-time; and when they are ready to re-enter the workforce or return to full-time, they take the "on-ramp" and they are back in the flow of traffic (the workforce). The reality is that many mothers do not identify with advice to take extended periods of time off from their jobs or reduce their schedules because their full-time paychecks are necessary to survival.

During my 30 years of motherhood, I have been able to stay at home with my kids for a minute portion of that time. After a divorce that plunged me into single motherhood, my finances were fairly dire. Even with regular child support payments, I barely scraped by. After remarriage to a man of modest means and adding child number three to the mix, I have worked outside the home in order to ensure that we have had a roof over our heads, cars in running order with gas in the tank, a refrigerator and pantry stocked with the essentials, clothes, shoes, and coats that fit, and doctors, dentists, and orthodontists paid for services rendered.

African American mothers have been largely ignored in the discourse of women's rights. Examining black women and feminism, journalist Renee Martin wrote that when Betty Friedan wrote the Feminine Mystique in 1963, she was *not* addressing women of color.[7] According to Martin, "white women were largely kept out of the workforce, but there were plenty of jobs for women of color as maids in their houses and nannies for their kids." For black mothers, the idea of working outside the home is a different conversation than the one in which their white counterparts engage.

In the book, *Mommy Wars*, Sydney Trent, an African American journalist and Senior Editor for *The Washington*

Post, wrote an essay on motherhood that gives a view into the culture of the African American mother.[8] Trent writes that an education and career for an African American woman has traditionally been viewed as "the Holy Grail that would uplift the race." Trent makes an interesting cultural observation that, as a mother of two, she rarely feels judged by blacks for working outside the home, but often feels judged by whites. Despite the changes in the lives of African American females, according to Trent, "Today, we continue to work, mostly out of need but also out of proud tradition and because there is no taboo among blacks against a woman saying that she wants to work…that she *likes* to work."

Trent is married to a white man whose mother didn't work outside the home, whereas Trent's own divorced mother was doubly-employed. In her essay, "What Goes Unsaid," Trent describes an underlying current within her husband's family of assumptions about her choice to work outside the home and how her choice impacts the quality of her mothering.

The spate of books, articles, and blogs on childrearing gives testament to various faces of motherhood; all of whom strive to be "good moms." Judith Warner describes stressed-out "helicopter moms" who engage in "total motherhood," referring to women who strive for perfectionism through controlling an exorbitant variety of aspects of their children's lives—issues that range from ant hills to mountains.[9] Warner writes, "Too many women in America are becoming sick with exhaustion and stressed as they try to do things that can't be—shouldn't be—done. We've become mothering perfectionists…a generation of control freaks…ever vigilant, ever devoted, ever in control."

These women's plates are overflowing because they have not removed some of the potatoes as they added the peas and carrots. Like a spinning plate atop a stick, mothers' lives spin out of control when they take on too much, shouldering the burden of blame when things go wrong. And something *always* goes wrong with kids in the house.

One mother told Warner how she felt like a failure when her toddler son needed emergency room treatment and he had to be held down to insert an IV. Admittedly, this woman was speaking of raw emotion; but failure as a mom? Unless this mom was grossly negligent in a way that resulted in him being rushed to the ER, one wonders why she would feel like a failure. My own son suffered from asthma as a toddler and the first time he was hospitalized for pneumonia, he had to be strapped down for IV insertion. As his mother, I cried for his pain, not because of anything I had failed to do. As for the description of "total motherhood," since I've been a member of both the low-income category and the middle-income category, I do not identify with the term "helicopter mom." I've hit exhaustion just trying to keep up, no hovering involved; just the day-to-day unrelenting realities of a mother of three.

Just one example of over-the-top mothering that has become a badge of honor is the evolution of children's birthday parties. Personally, I remember one birthday party that involved my friends. I was in the third grade and my older sister threw it for me. A lot has changed since then.

My daughter was invited to her first "friends" birthday party when she was four years old. I thought that was kind of young, so I stayed at the party rather than drop-and-go. What ensued was a veritable smorgasbord of activities with an abundance of Pre-K children in attendance. Polaroid pictures were taken of each child and inserted into

77

homemade frames as a take-home gift; kids were shuffled from the backyard for the piñata (which took a long while before giving way to the jabs of four-year-olds) to the craft table, and throughout the two-story house for a treasure hunt. As one of the parents who stayed with my four-year-old, let me describe the scene: utter chaos. And each child, except mine and one other child whose parent stayed, had cried at one point during the party. It was overload for the children, and an overwhelming expenditure of energy on the part of the birthday girl's mother.

Birthday parties have evolved even further from the one my daughter attended a decade ago, removing them from children's homes to venues replete with expensive bells and whistles. One mother told me about her child's birthday party with so much going on that there was no time to open the presents. My thought upon hearing this was: "Aww, the birthday boy didn't get to open his presents?"

When I planned my daughter's first "friends" birthday party, I recalled the Chaos Party. For her fifth birthday, we kept the guest list very small, we had musical chairs, pin-the-tail-on-the-donkey, Hot Potato, cake and ice cream, presents, and then "Home you go!" I felt instinctively that five-year-olds do not want to be at a three-hour-long party. They want some giggles, cake, and to watch the birthday girl open the present that they proudly helped pick out; and then they want their mommies or daddies (or grammies). The birthday girl felt special and loved, and no one cried.

There are countless "mom blogs" across the Internet, some of which are anonymous blogs with tales of shame and terror. Stories of shame for not being able to keep up with unrealistic expectations, or the terror of dealing with tantrum-throwing kids who echo the four-letter-words they hear their mamas utter under their breath, and the guilt for not enjoying every nanosecond that childrearing entails.

These moms post their rants anonymously, for to admit publicly that there are great expanses of time when they are bored out of their skulls, or that they feel some resentment toward their children, whose needs take precedence day and night, would make them feel like "bad mothers."

Again, if there were more support systems in place, perhaps being a mom would be less exhausting. But the fact remains that the majority of mothers shoulder most of the childrearing, household chores, and the invisible mental tasks of orchestrating family life.

Sheryl Sandberg's book, *Lean In,* advises women to lean into their careers in order to increase the number of women in leadership roles who would then be in a position to bring about family-friendly policies in the workplace.[10] With the U.S. the only industrialized nation without mandated paid maternity leave, one can see why women in leadership would be a boon for moms in the workplace. Sandberg's advice could be compared to The Talented Tenth concept, as described by W.E.B. DuBois in 1903. DuBois emphasized the need for higher education among the most able 10% of talented African Americans in order to develop the leadership capacity needed to bring about changes for black Americans. While there is merit in encouraging those who are able to "lean in" and develop their leadership capacities, this is not the reality for those without an adequate support system. How do we get more women into leadership roles when they don't have the support systems they need?

The book, *Getting to 50/50,* by Sharon Meers and Joanna Strober, calls for equity among two-parent households.[11] According to the authors, "While inequity can seep into marriage in many ways, the birth of children is the most common cause." While their book refers to the traditional family form—with marriages, husbands, and fathers—one can recognize the alliance of which they speak and extrapolate their advice to whatever kind of support system employed by a mother. The idea is that mothers cannot and should not shoulder all of the childcare load just because they possess two X chromosomes.

In fact, a mom gives her child a great gift in the form of a relationship with the child's father—or whoever is involved in the Parenting Partnership. Mothers tend to feel that they are the best at "all-things-childrearing" and insist on being in control because they do not trust others (dad or the other half of the Parenting Partnership) to do things the "right" way. This concept is referred to as "maternal gatekeeping." To walk out the door and leave one's child with your partner is to allow a special kind of relationship to flourish, built on alone time. It gives mom a break and it builds self-esteem in the parent/partner who is not normally "on call" (who may also buy into the belief that "mom does it best"). A deeper relationship between father (or partner) and child is fostered when they are left to their own devices. We all have our own ways of doing things; when mothers insist that it's their way or the highway, they can count on an imbalance in the childcare/household load.

Meers and Strober offer advice on how mothers can assert their needs in order to work toward a balanced relationship with shared responsibilities for household duties, as well as how mothers can assert their needs in the workplace. As a book geared toward two-parent families and mothers who have careers that allow them leeway to assert their needs, the authors' advice is sound. Unfortunately, flexible work schedules are not the norm. And more mothers than ever are flying solo with regard to parenting and household duties, either from lack of a partner or due to various arrangements that are not conducive to a 50/50 arrangement. For example, one mother describes how her husband travels frequently; thus, this woman flies solo a good deal of the time. When her husband is at home, she naturally wants him to have time with their kids. Asking him to sweep the floor or do the laundry would cut into that time, so she doesn't ask.

Navigating a 50/50 balance is extremely hard in certain families. Having two children from a previous marriage, I will always be a mother of three compared to my husband who is a biological father of one. When my husband was activated for military service after 9-11, I was rendered a single mom while he was gone. Years ago, his mother was married, younger, and healthy; whereas, my mother was widowed, older, and suffered significant health problems. Navigating all these inequities into some semblance of balance has been extremely difficult.

The faces of motherhood vary according to income, ethnicity, childrearing practices, and support systems. Mothers seem to be struggling despite being part of a two-parent household. How much harder is motherhood when pursued on one's own?

"When the day is done, the kids safely in bed,
No energy's left for the thoughts in her head...
Before the rise of the sun, she be up and back to it.
There's no other option. No one else to do it."
Tamara Sue Appelman, blogger

Chapter 9: Single Moms: From Grimaces to Grins

In Nathaniel Hawthorne's *Scarlet Letter*, set in the 1600s in
a repressive Puritan society, Hester Prynne is forced to
wear the letter "A" (for Adulteress) on her breast as a brand
of shame after she is found to be pregnant out-of-wedlock.
This was society's way of holding her accountable for her
transgression against their rules and expectations.

Almost 400 years later (in the mid-1980s), I had two
friends who became pregnant out-of-wedlock. Both rushed
into marriages because that was the expectation of society.
Very few people knew that both these young ladies were
pregnant when they uttered "I do" at the altar. Back then,
the idea of babies born to unmarried females was still cause
for embarrassment.

Fast forward to 1992 when Candice Bergen in the then-
popular TV series *Murphy Brown* starred as a single news
anchorwoman who gets pregnant and chooses to keep the
baby. *Time* magazine quoted Vice President Dan Quayle as
complaining that Murphy Brown, "a character who
supposedly epitomizes today's intelligent, highly paid
professional woman," was portrayed as "mocking the
importance of fathers by bearing a child alone, and calling
it just another lifestyle choice."[1] This same article referred
to the Murphy Brown character as glorifying unwed
motherhood.

As we face life in the 21st century, the stigma of an unwed mother has melted away. Gone are the days when single, pregnant women were coerced into shotgun weddings or giving up their babies for adoption. We find today a society that embraces single motherhood, as exemplified by the throwing of great big baby showers for these women. When a close friend became pregnant out-of-wedlock in the 1980s, we discussed the idea of a baby shower. We knew it would raise some eyebrows so we opted for a small, intimate shower with just a few family members and her closest friends. We've definitely come a long way in a couple of decades.

While I would never advocate the return to the days of the *Scarlet Letter,* nor to the days just a couple of decades ago when women were forced into marriage against their better judgment because of an out-of-wedlock pregnancy, I do suggest that we consider how the paradigm shift of "grimaces to grins" has affected the children involved. When a single woman becomes pregnant unexpectedly, will the father participate in the raising of the child? If the picture does not include a father, what kind of support network will there be to help the mother and her child through the ensuing 18+ years?

American society is not set up to support families who stray from the traditional form – mother/father/a kid or two. Unfortunately, single mothers and their children find themselves among the poorest sector of society in this country. According to the U.S. Census Bureau, 31.6% of households headed by single women lived in poverty in 2010, compared to 6.2% of married-couple households.[2] As a society, we lack the support systems such as quality, affordable daycare, fair pay standards, and guaranteed paid sick days which would help single mothers fight the pull of poverty. When a single mother lacks the support she needs and has to struggle to make ends meet, perhaps working more than one job, depositing her child in whatever kind of daycare she can patch together (sometimes quality, sometimes not), fighting poverty or near-poverty becomes an uphill battle. And everyone pays a price.

In the book, *Promises I Can Keep: Why Poor Women Put Motherhood Before Marriage*, sociologists Kathryn Edin and Maria Kefalas examine the role American society plays in encouraging teens to have sex and babies.[3] Edin and Kefalas talked in-depth with low-income mothers; they offer an intimate look at what motherhood means to these women and why so many American youth continue to have children before they can afford to take care of them. The results of their five-year, on-the-ground study show that the absence of infrastructure, education, and restrictions on reproductive and social services in inner city communities where they are most needed serves to encourage subsequent generations to keep having sex and babies. Despite the fact that this group of pre-teens/teenagers is so maligned in American public policy, they are faced with complacency from public figures who refuse to support programs which would help them.

On an emotional level, having a baby can meet the basic human need of "belonging," so integral to psychological well-being—something not always easy to find in inner city communities. Having a baby can also provide a compelling sense of purpose. The authors interviewed a young woman named Jen, "I didn't have nothing to go home for…nobody to take care of…now I have my son…I have him to go home for."

Like so many others, I became a single mom after a divorce. I married, had two kids, and got divorced when my sons were preschoolers. When single motherhood came knocking at my door, I entered the hamster wheel of life and I had to fight to keep my balance while running full speed ahead. Even with a father in the picture to pick up the children every other weekend, there's still the other 80% of days and nights where these little people depend completely on *your* energy to feed them, bathe them, check their homework, read them stories, pack their lunches, and tuck them into bed with hugs in hopes that is where they'll stay. And that's just one evening out of a week of evenings that look pretty much the same. Throw in a parent-teacher conference, feverish child, or a band recital, and you feel stretched beyond the breaking point. After all, how fast can one run in that hamster wheel?

Assuredly, there are situations where a child can be given a warm, loving home environment that leads to an emotionally strong adult with a high sense of self-esteem despite the lack of a participatory or present father. Increasingly, we find financially-stable women are choosing single motherhood after building solid careers and not finding a suitable mate. I have heard from single moms that fathers are irrelevant. This sentiment has contributed to the estimated $3.3 billion sperm donor industry.[4] Women can visit a sperm bank and modern science helps them achieve their goal of becoming mothers. Adoption is another pathway to single motherhood, although policies among adoption agencies vary.

According to renowned psychologist and founder of the Head Start program, Urie Bronfenbrenner, the single determinant for a child's emotional well-being is "one or two dependable caregivers who are crazy about the child."[5] Even though data from the Fragile Families and Child Well-being Study shows that children who grow up in single-mother homes fare worse than children born into married-couple homes in the areas of cognitive, behavioral, and health outcomes, the study points to family *stability* as more important than family *structure*.[6] This reinforces what Bronfenbrenner asserted with regard to a support system of dependable caregivers invested in the child's future over the long haul. Bronfenbrenner wrote that effective parenting depends on "role demands, stresses, and supports emanating from other settings...external factors (such as) flexibility of job schedules, adequacy of childcare arrangements, the presence of friends and neighbors who can help out in large and small emergencies, the quality of health and social services, and neighborhood safety." All these factors lead to the stability that experts point to in order to raise a well-adjusted child.

Life is not perfect. We often find ourselves in situations that are less than optimal. But we would do well to consider the necessary support structure needed for both mother and child.

"It doesn't matter who my father was;
it matters who I remember he was."
Anne Sexton, poet

Chapter 10: A Word about Fathers

Are fathers truly irrelevant? While it is clear that single
moms throw themselves into mothering their children with
as much energy as they can muster, it is also true that a
strong support system is needed which is too often lacking.
Just because a man fathers a child does not mean he will be
the kind of support that a mother or child needs. There are
a lot of deadbeat dads out there. There are dads who are
emotionally distant or abusive with their kids, and some
seem to do more damage than good. But there are equally
as many good dads out there. I was lucky enough to have
one.

There are people in my life who would disagree with my
sentiment that I had a good dad. And they would be
justified in feeling that way. I have heard stories of what
my older brothers and sisters went through at the hands of
my dad's physical abuse. My father subscribed too literally
to the adage "spare the rod, spoil the child." But he must
have tired by the time I came along (I'm the youngest),
because I only remember one such beating with a "switch"
(a thin branch cut from a tree).

I don't know what made my dad commit unspeakable hurts
against those he was supposed to love and protect. What I
do know is that he was there every day when I came home
from school, waiting with hot chocolate on cold days, and
we'd watch *Gilligan's Island* on TV. When I was sick and
bedridden, he would make me soup and bring me stack
upon stack of *Archie* comics. He was there when I was in
need of chauffeuring to dental appointments, school, or to
friends' homes. He taught me to drive defensively and play

checkers (his passion); we took long walks to pick wildflowers; and he often showed me the prized pigeons he raised. This was the dad I grew up with. He wasn't perfect, and I remember the bad stuff. But he was my dad, he was there, and I loved him.

I still remember my father's comment upon hearing about a woman who got pregnant out-of-wedlock without the baby's father in the picture, "I wouldn't have wanted to grow up without my father." He said this despite the fact that his own father was a raging alcoholic; an abusive man, who drank up the family's money instead of buying necessary items for his three children during the Depression era. I surmise that my father also experienced moments when he felt his father's love, despite the frailties and mistakes of the man he called Dad.

Mariel Hemingway, granddaughter of Ernest Hemingway (one of the greatest American writers of all time), expressed love for her father despite revealing that he was "inappropriately intimate" with her two older sisters (who were 7 and 11 years older than Mariel). She describes the alcohol-induced insanity that comprised her childhood in the documentary, *Running From Crazy*. Mariel felt deeply conflicted about revealing the secrets of her childhood because she loved her father (who died in 2000); but she wanted to shed light on her sisters' lives (one committed suicide at age 41; the other was addicted to drugs). Mariel says, "My dad was a wonderful human being…but alcoholism is a bad disease and you do f'ed up things."[1]

In my own family where my father was both perpetrator and victim, I have asked myself whether I'd have been better off without him in my life. While I am left with anger and sadness knowing the pain he inflicted behind closed doors on others, he was my dad. He didn't walk out the door and desert his family. He worked hard to support us, at mostly menial jobs. I've heard it said that we all have different parents. My oldest brother, who endured the brunt of my father's physical abuse, had a very different father than I did. We don't talk about my dad in my family. We abide by the code of silence that is practiced by many families with a history of abuse.

There are dads who inflict more harm than good on their kids. In cases such as these, it is likely that the child would adopt the sentiment that no dad would have been better than this kind of dad. I acknowledge that there are people who would be justified in feeling this way about my dad.

Lauri Burns described how her father's abuse stretched as far back as she could remember.[2] As an adult, Lauri learned about the cycle-of-abuse theory and realized that her father must have been a victim as a child also. So she chose to forgive him. As a result, her father came to terms with his own self-loathing and, at age 73, entered therapy to heal his own childhood wounds. Lauri received professions of deep remorse and love from her dad for the first time in her life. Lauri channeled her understanding of abused kids by becoming a foster mom, as well as founding *The Teen Project* (for kids who "age out" of the foster care system). By finding a purpose in her suffering, this helped Lauri to forgive her dad. She wrote, "Only a person who has tapped into their own pain to heal others would understand."

I join my voice to Lauri's, to Mariel's, and to my own father's when I say: for those of us with fathers who were crappy in the eyes of others, we found value in their presence in our lives. Do we wish they were better people? Hell yes. But that does not alter our love for our dads.

Statistics speak loudly on the importance of fathers in a child's life. High school drop-out rates are much higher for children growing up without their dads; and these statistics hold up along ethnic lines. Even when there are alternative support structures in place, for those who grew up not knowing their dads, they lamented that missing piece from their life puzzle.

When I asked Claire,* 24, who grew up without her father, if there was something she wishes her mom had done differently; she answered, "I wish she had made better choices. I wish she had gotten married before getting pregnant to ensure that there would be someone who wanted to stick around." When asked whether she would want a child of hers to grow up without knowing his or her dad, her answer was, "Never. That will not happen."

Samantha,* 30, spoke about the decisions made by her mom: "I definitely wish I could have grown up having a relationship with my dad…I remember it hit me hard when I was 11 years old; I remember thinking it wasn't fair. Then when I got much older, I felt a deep sadness." In an example of repeating patterns, Samantha gave birth out-of-wedlock to a son who has never met his father. I asked Samantha about her situation and if she would have done anything differently: "I would have waited to get pregnant until I got married to ensure that there would be someone there to support me and my child."

In the movie, *Mamma Mia,* one of the main characters, a 20-year-old woman who was raised by her mother and never met her biological father, tells her mom that growing up not knowing her father "…is crap!"[3] It appears that the statement has been simmering below the surface and comes out in the heat of the moment. Often, kids don't express their feelings to their moms for fear of hurting their feelings.

---

* Names have been changed.

According to author Janetta Rose Barras, women who grew up without their dads "were never given the language to express their pain or loss."[4] Barras says that the voices of children brought up without their fathers are often stifled. Their feelings are not given recognition or a name.

Regan,* 19, found a way to express her feelings about growing up without her biological dad. When prompted by a social networking site to name the one person she'd like to meet most in the world, she wrote, "my biological dad." This allowed her to express herself without hurting her mom.

In the documentary by Janks Morton, *Dear Daddy*, young women were given a chance to voice their feelings about their missing or nonparticipatory dads.[5] In heart-rending fashion, these women wrote letters to the fathers who abandoned them or who did not show enough interest in them to be a consistent, dependable presence in their lives as they grew up. Eighteen-year old Jasmine, whose taped reading of her letter went viral on YouTube, reads with a voice steeped in anger and pain, telling her father that she hopes he burns in hell because he was not there for her and her single mother. Another young lady, Imoni, age 16, whose father was in and out of her life as she grew up, says that she still loves him; she says this with a forced smile and tears streaming from her eyes.

Morton's documentary highlights some startling facts; teenage girls who are raised without their fathers are more likely to suffer from depression, drop out of school, and have other behavioral problems. Because these girls will seek physical male contact more often than girls who had an intact relationship with their dads, there is also a higher prevalence of teenage pregnancy among this segment of the

---

* Name has been changed.

population. Later in Morton's documentary, we hear from Jasmine's mother, Tina, who relates that she also did not grow up with her dad in her life (another example of the repeating cycle).

One young woman I interviewed, Debbie,* age 30, was sexually abused at a young age. Debbie said, "If I'd had a dad, he would have protected me." Whether or not this is a true statement does not matter as much as the sentiment. This young woman felt vulnerable and unprotected. When asked whether she thinks a father is a necessary part of a healthy upbringing for a child, Debbie answered, "Yes, definitely."

Then there's Mark,* 27, who said, "If I'd had a dad, my character attributes would be different; I'd have had someone to challenge me." Mark related his story from the men's transient hotel where he was struggling to survive. He said that when he was very young, "I remember a feeling of rejection; that my father had rejected me." By age 16, Mark said he was displaying deviant behavior and had "lots of conflict in my life." When asked if he would want any child of his to grow up without a dad, Mark answered, "I wouldn't wish that on anyone." Mark says he doesn't blame his mom for his troubles; and as he says this, his voice trails off.

In contrast, children who were raised without their fathers but with a strong support system had a different attitude about their upbringing. In my interview with Claire (introduced earlier), she indicated that she was raised by her single mom in the home of her grandparents. In addition, there were many aunts, uncles, and cousins who helped to provide a strong network for her and her mom. Claire does not remember feeling, as a child, that

---

* Names have been changed.

something was missing from her life. And she seems to have a high sense of self-esteem, which she credits to the strong network of extended family she was surrounded by as she grew up.

It is important to note the differences in the experiences of Debbie and Mark versus Claire with regard to family stability and the support systems that were in place (or lacking) for their single moms. For Claire, the fact that her grandparents and extended family provided a strong network made a huge difference in her life.

American culture touts the traditional family form as being ideal or best; at the same time it denounces alternate forms of family life. One alternate form of family life involves gay couples raising children together. According to Timothy Biblarz, co-author of a review of children raised by same-sex couples, "On most all of the measures that we care about, self-esteem, school performance, social adjustment and so on, (these children) seem to be doing just fine and, in most cases, are statistically indistinguishable from kids raised by married moms and dads on these measures."[6]

In other words, it is the stability of a strong support network in place for the child that is important, whether that is two dads, two moms, two grandparents, or a mom and extended family. Stability trumps structure.

"Friendship is essentially a partnership"
Aristotle

Chapter 11: The Parenting Partnership

It takes a combination of the "big three" to raise a child –
Time, Energy, and Money. Realistically speaking, it is the
rare person who has enough of all three while embracing
solo parenting, holding down a job, and carrying out the
demands of everyday life.

Research shows that children born into married-couple
households fare better than those born to unwed parents in
terms of cognitive, behavioral, and health outcomes.[1] The
reason for this is that a Parenting Partnership provides a
strong, dependable support system for the child. Having a
partner helps to alleviate some of the stress, provides built-
in support, and cuts down on the number of roles a mother
must fulfill. Dealing with external factors such as job
schedules and childcare is easier when there is a Parenting
Partnership in the mix.

Few people realize the long road that parenthood traverses.
Eighteen-plus years is a very long time period to exude
enormous amounts of one's time, energy, and money.
Without a dependable back-up person, who will take care
of the child when Mom is sick? Or if she's laid up in the
hospital? These questions are best answered in advance of
the need.

Our society continues to focus on the traditional form of
family; however, there are many alternatives to the "norm"
that work just fine. There are people who will argue this
point, but I believe that as long as there is a viable, long-
term Parenting Partnership that provides the child with a
strong support system of love and caring, then what that

partnership actually looks like is not as important as the result. In Hillary Clinton's book, *It Takes a Village*, she states that "what a family looks like to the outside is not as important as whether adults understand what children need to develop positively."[2] Understanding that children need a strong, long-term network of loving adults who have generous amounts of time, energy, and patience is essential.

All kinds of deviations from the traditional family form exist. One example I observed is a homosexual male and a lesbian female, friends who decided to procreate together in order to achieve parenthood. The results: two healthy children. Mom and Dad don't live together but they share in the parenting of these two children. The children created by this nontraditional union are loved and supported because there's a stable, long-term Parenting Partnership.

There is no question that a child benefits most from an intact, healthy mother/father relationship throughout childhood, adolescence, and into adulthood. But the underlying factor is that this setting provides a child with a built-in support network of two people who are crazy about him or her; who have the patience to endure years of time/energy-drain; and who will be there to back each other up in the Parenting Partnership. Even with just one child, the drain on the "big three" is, at times, unimaginable. The mental and physical energy expended when dealing with a cranky two-year-old or a hormonal 15-year-old can feel overwhelming. Not to mention the unrelenting commitments with doctors, dentists, school functions, homework...the list really is endless.

Myself, I am grateful for the presence and partnership with my children's fathers. I am referring to two men since I have children from two marriages. I had two sons with my first husband and when we split, we continued the Parenting Partnership. As our sons grew to be teenagers, I felt that the rebelliousness that was a natural part of that stage needed the firm hand of their biological father *in the home*. This is not to say that my second husband, their stepfather, wasn't doing the best that he knew how. But there was a threshold over which their stepfather would not cross. Thus, their biological dad and I came up with an arrangement where they were able to spend more blocks of time with him. As much as it pained me to give up more of my time with my sons, I felt that it was the right decision. Looking back, I still think it was a good decision; and I'm grateful that their dad was there for them.

In my current marriage of 20+ years, my husband and I are still raising our teenage daughter. We have found that there is a difference in how our daughter listens to her father versus how she listens to me. Since I'm at home more, I tend to handle the day-to-day issues. Once, when there was a significant issue at hand, our daughter accepted her father's edict in a way that she was unwilling or unable to accept it from me. And that's really the point. With a Parenting Partnership, there is another person's voice at the ready. Someone who can bring a different perspective to whatever situation is at hand. Someone who loves the child and is invested in his or her future. If Mom fails in bringing about the desired response, then Dad gives it a try. And vice versa. This can be the tactic in any Parenting Partnership, no matter what that partnership looks like. And this includes gay and lesbian Parenting Partners.

According to Benjamin Siegel, Boston University School of Medicine professor of pediatrics, three decades of research supports the idea that gay parents form Parenting Partnerships that produce happy, well-adjusted kids.[3] In a report published by the American Academy of Pediatrics, Siegel wrote, "Many studies have demonstrated that children's well-being is affected much more by their relationships with their parents, their parents' sense of

96

competence and security, and the presence of social and economic support for the family than by the gender or the sexual orientation of their parents."[4] This speaks directly to research that emphasizes that family *stability* and support systems are more important than family *structure*.

As a part of Motherhood Catechism dogma, females learn that becoming a mother "should" be a part of their life plan, whether they approach it early or later in life. But what's missing from the "lesson plan" is the fact that a child's well-being depends upon stability and built-in support systems. We do women a disservice when we tell them that motherhood is an essential component of their lives in all situations. If the support structure doesn't exist, women shouldn't be cajoled, counseled or prodded into pursuing motherhood. There are many other paths to a happy life.

Chapter 12: Significant Costs

News flash! Having children is expensive! Okay, you
already knew that. But did you know that the annual cost
of childcare in much of the United States parallels the cost
of one year of college? According to ChildCare Aware of
America, the average annual cost for center-based care for
an infant is higher than a year's tuition and related fees at a
four-year public college in 35 states and the District of
Columbia.[1] That's right folks, by the time you put junior
through a few years of childcare, you could have put him
through the equal number of years of college. And that's
just one part of a much bigger picture.

Add up the cost of diapers, formula, commercial baby food,
toys, clothes, dentists, doctors, braces, trumpets, soccer
uniforms, karate lessons – the list is absolutely endless.
Oh, and that's just through adolescence. Consider also the
plethora of activities related to the culmination of junior
high and high school. My daughter handed me a list of five
events related to the end of junior high, informing me that
three new dresses would do nicely. And shoes. And
jewelry. And a haircut. You get the point. The high
school years bring prom clothes, class rings, cell phones,
and exorbitantly expensive senior-year photo packages, just
to name a few. And don't forget the increase in auto
insurance that accompanies that birthday we call "sweet
sixteen."

The actual number that captures all of the above is as
follows: according to the USDA, the agency that annually
tallies how much families spend to raise children from birth

to age 18, middle-class parents of a child born in 2010 can expect to spend more than a quarter-of-a-million dollars in the child's first 18 years (excluding college).[2] This number is up from the previous year—which was a bargain at $222,360.[3]

When it comes to college, many parents feel that they *owe* their child a college education. The U.S. government happens to view it that way, as evidenced by FAFSA rules (the government's arm for financial aid for college). I happen to feel that my motherly duty includes a good upbringing and a good start at life. Footing the whole bill for college is not in that category. I helped both my sons with college costs. One son ended up with a hefty college loan that he'll be paying off for years to come.

The economy in the U.S. has changed in a way that today's generation needs a college education more than ever before. Gone are the days when it was easy for someone who opted out of college to find a job capable of supporting a family, with a nice little pension upon retirement. Due to the exodus of so many jobs overseas, as well as advances in technology, the U.S. job market is comprised largely of service-oriented jobs, leaving fewer opportunities for those who opt out of college but still want to grab onto some version of the American dream.

As the mantra goes, you can't put a price tag on joy. There are parents who insist that a life without children is a life without fulfillment (a tenet common to Motherhood Catechism). According to a study published in *Psychological Science,* a journal of the Association for Psychological Science (APS), parents create idealized pictures of parental joy as a way to justify the huge investment that kids require.[4] There is a psychology term for this type of justification of one's actions—cognitive dissonance—which is a defense mechanism to justify one's choices and beliefs in the face of conflicting evidence.

The APS puts their findings into a historical perspective by explaining that in earlier times, kids had significant "economic value" and they didn't cost that much to raise. America's landscape has changed dramatically since the days when family farms were plentiful and families with many children equated to more hands for performing chores. Also gone, thankfully, are the days when children brought home paychecks from factory jobs. With the passing of the Fair Labor Standards Act in 1938, children are no longer allowed at jobs that jeopardize their well-being, health, or educational opportunities.

As the economic value of children diminished and costs escalated, "the belief that parenthood is emotionally rewarding has gained currency," according to the APS. In that sense, parental joy can be viewed as a sort of modern psychological phenomenon.

Daniel Gilbert offers an explanation for society's need to create an idealized picture of parental joy in his book *Stumbling upon Happiness*.[5] Gilbert borrows the term super-replicator from biology—a process where genes that contribute to the proliferation of a species replicate and become more prevalent in future generations—and applies it to what he calls the "belief transmission game." Gilbert asserts that certain beliefs can be super-replicators if they preserve the social system that allows the belief to be transmitted or passed along to the next generation. Gilbert gives two examples of beliefs that are super replicators: money and children. A fairly common belief in the U.S. is that money brings happiness; which is very important because it helps to preserve its capitalist economy. However, this belief flies in the face of accuracy when one considers the number of wealthy people who are unhappy despite their amassed riches. It seems that once one has enough money to satisfy one's needs (e.g., food, clothing, a home, etc.), that adding more money to a person's pocket may not necessarily increase happiness—the economic term for this is declining marginal utility. When it comes to the belief that children bring happiness, according to Gilbert, tagging an experience as joyous where the vast majority of your time is spent in repetitious chores, catering to people who will take decades to *maybe* feel gratitude for all you've done for them, doesn't quite ring with accuracy either. But the belief that children bring happiness ensures the survival of the human race and the flourishing of various cultures. Society's brokers in the belief transmission game are our moms, aunts, uncles, hair dressers, and co-workers, among others. It seems that everyone, from our loved ones to the media, gets in on the game.

Even though the financial and emotional costs are greater than some parents bargain for, it is not until after becoming a parent that this becomes abundantly apparent. Without sounding too much like an investment broker, let me introduce the idea that for all I've invested in my children, I have expected a certain return on my investment (ROI). That ROI comes in the form of respect, honor, and the kind of unconditional love that I have dished out for years on end. After spending my time, energy, and money in support of raising my children to adulthood, I freely admit that I expect to be rewarded with caring, responsible, and independent individuals who love me and take care with my feelings.

There is no way to enumerate all of the financial costs of parenthood. The USDA has used different methodologies, ranging from money actually spent on children for housing, food, and clothing, to lost income opportunities borne by

101

at-home parents who forego paid jobs outside the home in favor of caring for the children.

It is equally difficult to tabulate the "opportunity cost" of having kids. An economic term, the opportunity cost of a choice is the value of other foregone alternatives that involve other uses of one's resources, resulting in varying degrees of accomplishment or pleasure.

Studies that compare adults *with* children to adults *without* children show that those *with* children experience lower emotional well-being, suffer from depression, and have unhappier marriages. It is important to clarify the difference between couples without children *by choice* and couples who are unable to conceive. Of the latter group, there is more stress as a result of wanting but being unable to have children; therefore, those marriages understandably may be unhappier and have a higher ratio of divorce.

The decrease in happiness for couples with kids can be attributed to less time to focus on each other's needs as well as their own, the relentless stress that having children brings, and resentment that can build when the balance is off with regard to orchestrating family life. There can be a constant struggle or negotiation over who does the cooking, cleaning, and grocery shopping; who schedules the child's doctor/dental/orthodontist appointments; who checks the homework, ensures that the children are bathed, and that there's an adequate supply of clothes that fit. Everyone gets tired and cranky, moms, dads, kids. It's all very unsexy.

Too often, we hear of marriages that break up after 25 years, even 40 years. Somewhere along the journey, these couples lost each other. According to the National Survey on Family Growth, first marriages have a 50% chance of the union lasting until the 20th anniversary. [6] Factors

affecting this statistic are religion and education—both
with positive impacts on a lasting union—as well as other
factors such as age at marriage, ethnicity, and whether
biological children were brought into the equation. Studies
show that after the first child comes along, marital
satisfaction drops in 70% of couples. A Philadelphia
divorce attorney, Dorothy Phillips said, "More than half the
matters in my office are parents in their 30s and early 40s
with young kids."[7]

These statistics point to the fact that the institution of
parenthood can be a factor in divorce in some instances.
However, we should never blame a child for a broken
marriage. Blaming a child for a broken marriage is like
blaming her for the terrible twos or for the trials of
teenager-hood. We bring these children into our lives and
we should not be surprised when our lives are turned upside
down. And yet, this realization of the topsy-turvy effect of
parenthood escapes a great many parental prospects. A
friend once asked me, "Why didn't you tell me how much a
child would change my life?" My answer: "Because you
wouldn't have believed me."

Time and again, I have offered subtle hints of this
impending lifestyle overhaul, only to have glowing
pregnant friends nod and smile. No one thinks it will affect
them so drastically. I once heard a pregnant woman say
that she planned to fit the baby into hers and her husband's
lifestyle instead of the other way around. My response was
to smile and fight my impulse to shout, "Hah! Little do
you know!" and let out a sinister cackle. In one year's
time, this woman's child went through multiple fevers,
coughs, sleepless nights, a problem with weight gain, and a
biting stage; to which this mom—who holds a top
management position—has dashed from work to pick up
her biting, coughing, feverish child and trash the rest of the

plans for her workday. This baby had his mom's number in utero. As do most babies.

With regard to happy marriages that last until death parts them, I will note here that most of the absolute hardest times in my marriage are attributed to parenthood. Again, this is no one's fault; and there is no blame to be laid. I only strive for frankness. In the first 19 years of my current marriage, my husband and I sought counseling three times: the first to deal with stepfamily issues; the second when my sons were teenagers; and the third time as our daughter entered her teenage years. With the help of counseling, we have navigated some significant hurdles.

I live in constant vigil of the stability of my marriage. I know that the strains of parenthood have taken its toll on us and will continue to tug at the seams of our marriage. Some of the relationship casualties have been less time, energy, and the quibbling over who will take care of what with regard to our child. Our opportunities to get away for quiet interludes together are few and far between. Once, when we had an explosive issue that needed discussing, we jumped into our car and drove to a nearby parking lot to be out-of-earshot of our daughter so that we would have the necessary privacy.

Not dealing with issues in the manner in which they need to be dealt with can be hazardous to the health of any relationship. I call this the "lumpy rug effect." Sweeping things under the rug does *not* resolve anything and those lumpy rugs lie in wait to trip you up in the future. Unfortunately, it is the absence of time and energy to work through issues that can eat away at relationships. Add to this the lack of time and privacy to engage in "couple" activities, such as lovemaking, unhurried talks about goals and what's important in life, and it is no surprise that there can be a gradual decline in the closeness a couple feels once they become parents.

With all my heart, I hope that my marriage stands the test of time and children. Would I have given up the chance to raise any of my three children? No. But it has been a steady uphill climb for my current 20+ year marriage; and the apex is not yet in sight. As we continue our ascent with a hormonal teenager in our midst, we know that each step must be taken carefully. For in the end, we want to beat the odds that have been stacked against us.

The sacrifices that are made in the name of parenthood are significant; and if we lose ourselves or our mates in the process, it is tough to justify all the costs.

Page intentionally left blank

Part III

Decisions, Decisions!

"Life is all about choices
and taking control over the things we can."
Dr. Ellen Walker, author/psychologist

Chapter 13: Planning or Preventing Motherhood

In the U.S., you do not need a license to become a mother.
Women just need the biological apparatus and the laws
protect their rights to their children. Philosophically
speaking, however, one could contend that motherhood is
more of a privilege rather than a right. It is a *privilege* to
take on responsibility for the life of another human being.
One may want to have a child, but does this desire eclipse
the needs of all others? No child asks to be brought into
this world. Thus, it is up to procreating adults to make
good decisions.

According to Dr. Jean Twenge—who coined the term
"Generation Me" to describe a combination of late Gen-Xs
and Gen-Ys born in the 1970s, 80s, and 90s—Generation
Me has grown up believing that it is more important to do
your own thing than conform to the group.[1] While the
Baby Boomers started the "question authority" wave, and
the accompanying sexual revolution, Generation Me has
taken it to the next level. According to Twenge, "The
current generation of procreative adults feels a sense of
entitlement that previous generations did not feel."
They've been instilled with the belief that expressing
oneself is a basic right, and this sense of expressing oneself
extends to sexual behaviors. Twenge quotes her master's
thesis which analyzed the sexual behaviors of 269,649
young people over four decades. According to Twenge,
"Boomers started having sex in college while GenMe
started having sex in high school...'hooking up' became a
term to describe sex between two people who don't

necessarily have any foreseeable future or hint of commitment."

Statistics show that almost 50% of all pregnancies in the U.S. are unplanned.[2] Narrowing the discussion to women between the ages of 18-29, that number jumps to 70%.[3] And for teens, 82% of all pregnancies are unplanned.[4] Which means that consideration of the wants and needs of others begins before conception, and extends to the decision of whether to keep the baby. Each individual needs to make the decision that feels right. No one can dictate to another person what the decision should be, although many people feel justified in doing so. At a time when effective birth control is both legal and readily available, it is feasible that unwanted or unplanned pregnancies could be reduced through education and an understanding of the life-long ramifications for both mother and child.

Striving to do what is right by any child requires responsible decisions, and this starts with the decision to engage in sexual intercourse with a person with whom one can envision a possible parenting partnership. And if this is not the case, then using an appropriate birth control method (before, during, or after sexual intercourse) makes sense. There is a plethora of options available to the 21st century woman. Abstinence is a viable and responsible option as well; although it is so hard to "sell" this form of birth control when American media hurls sexual innuendos at its populace at every opportunity.

Setting aside the debate of pro-life versus pro-choice for a minute, let's examine the realities of today's American society that includes casual sex as the norm. That casual sex is a part of mainstream American culture is an undeniable fact. Sexual innuendoes are a part of popular television shows, songs, video games, and movies. It seems that every marketing campaign contains an element of the battle cry, "Sex sells!" I've observed commercials for mops, car insurance, and sandwiches with sexual innuendos. A sexy sandwich? The barrage of sexual images that enters our homes through multiple channels is astounding; right into the hands and minds of impressionable young people.

It is understandable, therefore, that the teen birth rate in the United States is three times higher than every other developed country in the world.[5] According to a December 2012 Planned Parenthood Fact Sheet, 30% of American women become pregnant before the age of 20 – that's three in every ten young females.[6] Are there ten females living in your neighborhood? If so, can you imagine three of them becoming pregnant before they turn 20 years old?

In response to teen birth statistics, the American Academy of Pediatrics (AAP) issued a recommendation in November 2012 that pediatricians treating teenage girls should consider writing prescriptions for the morning-after pill to keep on hand "just in case."[7] This came on the heels of a recommendation from the American College of Obstetricians & Gynecologists (ACOG) that all birth control pills be made available over the counter. The Food & Drug Administration agreed with ACOG in the case of emergency contraception (aka the morning-after pill), as evidenced by its approval of over-the-counter sales of the "Plan B" morning-after pill with no age limits in 2011. This decision was overruled in December 2012 by the Health & Human Services Secretary at that time (Kathleen Sebelius), thereby reversing the FDA's decision and making it federal policy that girls under 17 needed a prescription to obtain emergency contraception. The AAP, ACOG and the Society for Adolescent Health and Medicine joined forces to denounce Sebelius's action. As this topic continues to evolve, in April 2013, a Federal judge in New York reversed the age restriction issued by HHS Secretary Sebelius; a news release issued by the FDA on April 30, 2013,[8] stated that the FDA approved Teva Women's Health, Inc. to market Plan B One-Step for use without a prescription for women 15 years of age and older.

As quoted earlier, 50% of all pregnancies in the United States are unplanned, with much higher rates for teens and women in their 20s. Following are factors that contribute to the high number of unplanned pregnancies:

Education – Schools get involved in educating kids on some of the basics of health education; otherwise the job of sex education is up to parents. As evidenced by birth rate statistics, young people are *not* receiving the information they need. Below are educational tools that could serve either as a springboard for discussion between parent and child, or as a means of self-help for women endeavoring to understand their bodies and the host of birth control options available to them. If they don't know what kind of birth control exists, they are powerless to utilize them:

- A great book is *Our Bodies, Ourselves,* first published over 40 years ago; written by women for women.[9] This book was given to me as a teenager and I've shared an updated version with my own daughter. Suffice it to say, a copy of this book will remain on my bookshelf for the rest of my life.
- The Internet has plenty of accurate information when it comes to planning or prevention of pregnancy. One good website is Bedsider.org – a birth control support network operated by the National Campaign to Prevent Teen & Unplanned Pregnancy. Their mantra: *"We believe knowledge is power. We believe babies are best when you're ready."*[10] The National Campaign to Prevent Teen & Unplanned Pregnancy has an option to sign up

for emails of an educational nature. I'm signed up and receive their regular updates.

- Planned Parenthood's website is an excellent educational tool on this topic. It has options such as: "Info for Teens," "Tools for Parents," "Tools for Educators," and a "Live Chat" option that facilitates a confidential discussion with a health educator (including a link on their home page that says "Worried? Had Unprotected Sex? Chat Now").[11] In addition, Planned Parenthood has a Latino Outreach Initiative since Latinos in the U.S. suffer disproportionately from sexually transmitted diseases; statistics show that they are least likely to be insured, making it difficult to get the sexual and reproductive healthcare they need. By 2035, it is estimated that one-third of all American youth will be Latino; Planned Parenthood serves Latino communities in need of service, education and advocacy efforts that reflect the needs and voices of Latinas, their families, and communities. See below for information on access to a Planned Parenthood health center near you.

Lack of Access – For teens, access is the number one barrier to effective birth control. For some, it is lack of understanding available options.

- Planned Parenthood is a good resource for women of all ages, especially teens, who can obtain confidential birth control services at a reasonable cost. There are offices throughout the U.S. Call their toll free number (800-230-PLAN) to find a local office near you. On a personal note, Planned Parenthood is where I obtained my first gynecological exam and birth control services as a teenager. I will always be eternally grateful that their confidential services were available to me.

113

- As of April 2013, any female or male who is 15 years or older can obtain emergency contraception (aka the morning-after pill) without a prescription (must have proof of age). Those under 15 can obtain emergency contraception with a prescription, which should be obtained in advance (as recommended by the American Academy of Pediatrics). Since this FDA approval is still relatively new (and has fluctuated due to legal maneuvering), some pharmacies are misinformed about age restrictions; this will change with time. To locate a local pharmacy that carries it, use the Pharmacy Locator option at www.planbonestep.com.[12]

High Cost
- Beginning in August 2012, health coverage laws took effect requiring most new and renewing health insurance plans to begin covering a broad array of women's preventive health services, most notably coverage of FDA-approved contraception, at no upfront cost. According to Kathleen Sebelius, who was Health and Human Services Secretary at that time, "Surveys showed that more than half the women in this country delayed or avoided preventive care because of its cost." This measure equates to improved healthcare for women and a reduction in unplanned pregnancies. As this book goes to press, outcomes from the Supreme Court case of Hobby Lobby v. Sebelius are unfolding, affecting which companies must offer all FDA-approved contraception at no upfront cost.[13]
- As mentioned above, Planned Parenthood offers low-cost birth control options, as well as other health services for both women and men (e.g., cholesterol and diabetes screening, cancer screening, including prostate and testicular

screening for men, testing for STDs, etc.). The list of general health care services varies by location.

Religion

- The Catholic Church prohibits use of artificial birth control, even within marriage. However, the majority of Catholics consider this point optional, as highlighted by a Pew Forum study that found only 11% of Catholics have three or more children,[14] a far cry from the stereotypical large Catholic families that pre-date reliable, legal birth control methods. If we look back to the Second Vatican Council (1962-65), we find that Pope Paul VI appointed a special commission to look into the subject of artificial birth control. That commission issued a recommendation to allow artificial birth control within marriage. In 1968, Pope Paul VI condemned artificial birth control *against* the recommendation of the commission. It was at this time that some theologians began to question "papal infallibility." And the average Catholic obviously questions it as well, resulting in much smaller families.
- There are numerous religions that condemn abortion, although only a handful disapprove of preventive forms of birth control. For example, Hinduism views family planning as an ethical good, drawn from the Dharma (Hindu doctrine) that emphasizes the need to act for the sake of the good of the world, and the belief that producing more children than one (or the environment) can support goes against Hindu code.[15]

Despite these issues, there are countless options for preventing pregnancy. The following is not meant to be an exhaustive list; only the highlights:

- Number one and 100% effective: abstinence.

- Before: Non-barrier, e.g., the Pill (99% effective if taken as directed, drops to 91% effective if *not* taken as directed, i.e., taking it on an erratic schedule/forgetting or taking an antibiotic while on the pill); implanted contraception such as an IUD or rod; or sterilization for a female or her partner. According to a 2010 report issued by HHS's Centers for Disease Control and Prevention, the most common methods of birth control are the oral contraceptive pill and female sterilization.[16]
- During: Barrier, e.g., condoms, diaphragm, sponge, cervical cap.
- After: Emergency Contraceptive Pills (ECPs, a.k.a., the morning-after pill) can be taken after sexual intercourse to prevent pregnancy, and are most effective if taken in the first 24 to 72 hours. According to ACOG, scientifically speaking, ECPs (e.g., *Plan B One-Step* or *Ella)* are *not* abortifacients (abortion pill) since they do not terminate a pregnancy.[17] "ECPs function primarily, if not exclusively, by inhibiting ovulation, thereby preventing fertilization from occurring." Further, "there is no evidence that UPA EC affects implantation." (UPA is the drug ulipristal acetate, used in the ECP *Ella*.) Princeton's Dr. James Trussell, a leading researcher for emergency contraception (EC), notes that in clinical trials with women with a Body Mass Index of 26 or higher (optimal is <25), "pregnancy rates were no different than if they hadn't used EC at all."[18] This is important to keep in mind when striving to maintain one's health as well as the efficacy of EC. The body is a veritable ecosystem, where different parts interact according to the balance we provide for it.

No discussion of preventing motherhood would be complete without a discussion of abortion. While abortion is not considered a birth control option, it is a form of preventing motherhood. There are two options for abortion: Medication Abortion (medication taken to end an early pregnancy—up to about 9 weeks), 97% effective; or In-Clinic Abortion Procedure, 100% effective. This subject was also touched upon in Chapter 3, stating that up until the early 1800s, abortion before quickening was not illegal; and became illegal because of the high risk of infection to patients during surgical procedures. Chapter 3 also explored Bible passages that refer to the death of a fetus (viewed as property versus a life). Abortion is legal due to *Roe v. Wade (1973)*; and as of mid-2013, laws in 14 of the 50 United States did *not* include a parental involvement requirement for a minor to have an abortion.[19] Of the 25 states with a parental involvement requirement, all *25* allow a judge to excuse that requirement. One state stipulates that a grandparent, aunt, uncle or sibling at least 25 years old can give permission. Other states have exclusions to parental involvement including cases of abuse. These laws continue to evolve.

Where do parents figure into all of the above? Honesty is a great place to start. However, honesty will probably go in one direction so long as a child feels she will be judged. Some parents feel that by talking with a teen about birth control, they are giving them permission to have premarital sex. That said, parents are greeted with sobering statistics about how many kids will experiment with sex while in high school (in 2009 that number was 46%); many parents may even harbor an unconscious assumption that their child will be a part of those statistics. In the larger context, there must be ongoing conversations about self-esteem, sexually-transmitted diseases, and the fact that the only form of birth control that is 100% effective is abstinence. Discussion about all the "what-if's" would be a good reality check that could help teens exercise good judgment with regard to their bodies. Females must be educated about the long road

117

and realities of motherhood; they deserve protection and honesty so that they can navigate the mantra they hear from peers: "Everybody's doing it!"

A poll conducted in June 2012 of 1,000+ teens (ages 15-18) and their parents revealed a huge discrepancy with regard to the job parents feel they are doing holding crucial conversations with their kids.[20] The three areas of focus were: How to say "no" to sex; Healthy versus unhealthy relationships; and Birth control methods. Overwhelmingly, parents thought they were doing a better job of communicating than their kids thought. Teens who participated in the poll either had not heard much from their parents on these subjects or they had no plans of talking with their parents on these topics. If we are to stem the tide of unplanned pregnancies in America, parents *must* do a better job of holding these conversations—whether teens are enthusiastic about having these crucial conversations with parents or not.

A wonderful website for kids as well as parents is "Students Against Destructive Decisions" (www.sadd.org) whose mission is peer-to-peer education about destructive decisions such as underage drinking, drug use, impaired or distracted driving, bullying, sexual activity, and teen suicide. Many high schools have SADD chapters where students can get involved. Whatever avenue a parent chooses, the important point is to choose an avenue of communication with one's child. Ignoring the issue does not make it go away.

Sascha's* mom was a "poster mom" when it came to encouraging her to think carefully about having sex and the consequences of such decisions. Her mom encouraged her to abstain from having sex until she really thought she was

---

* Name has been changed

ready, and to come to her if she felt the need for birth control. Sascha's mom refrained from setting up expectations for her life; she always said, "You have to do what's best for you." Sascha *did* go to her mom when she was 18 for birth control.

Since an unplanned pregnancy is not something I want my own daughter to experience if possible, the topics of sex education, relationships, and birth control are ones I have honestly addressed with her and will continue to do so. I wish for this kind of communication for all females. In fact, my teenage daughter helped me develop the following section based on what she has heard among her peers.

On a topic I call "mythbusters" (or urban legends), I would like to state that:
- Yes, Virginia, you can get pregnant the first time you have sex; whether it's your very first time or your 100th, it only takes one time (egg meets sperm and—voila!). I personally know women who can attest to this very basic biological fact.
- No, the birth control pill will *not* keep you from getting pregnant if you forget to take it, even if you only forget it once; you must abstain from sex or take other precautions until you get your next period, then go through another complete cycle of pills (remember that the effectiveness drops significantly if not taken as prescribed).
- Yes, certain medications render the birth control pill useless—you *will* ovulate if you are on antibiotics and the pill at the same time—either abstain from sex or use other precautions until you get your next period and take your next full cycle of pills.
- Yes, condoms do break—in which case, emergency contraception is an option.
- No, "pulling out" before the male ejaculates will *not* protect you from pregnancy. A small amount of semen is emitted *during* sex; see the below statistic for how many

millions of sperm are in an average ejaculation. Sperm have a job to do, and once released into your vagina, they're on a no-holds-barred" race to your eggs.
- Yes, abstinence is a viable option in this sex-crazed 21st century world of ours.
- No, it is *not* true that having sex within seven days of having your period is "safe." This particular myth came straight from the mouths of babes—my babe, my daughter—who has heard it countless times since she was in 7th grade, and has continued to hear it throughout her high school years. At this writing, she heard it "just the other day."
- For this next one—that you cannot get pregnant if you have sex while a woman is on her period (another myth my daughter has heard at school) ——I called in the big guns by consulting my OB/Gyn of 20+ years, who said, "Although there is some truth to the myth about not conceiving if intercourse occurs during menses, the problem is that not all bleeding is the result of menstruation, e.g., what if mid-cycle spotting is thought to be the period in a woman with irregular periods (oops!). The menses is anywhere from 7 to 14 days prior to ovulation; and the egg is viable for ~24-36 hours and sperm live 3-4 days in the uterus. On top of everything, sometimes, in medicine not all things can be explained."
- Finally, no, the rhythm method is not a reliable method of birth control. I am living proof.

In addition to the above "mythbusters," listed below are some facts from Mayo Clinic about certain conditions that lower a man's sperm count, such as:
-   Medical: certain infections, hormonal imbalance, certain medications, to name a few;
-   Environmental: exposure to industrial chemicals or radiation, overheating of the testicles (e.g., soaking in a hot sauna, excessive bike-riding which warms the testicles).

- <u>Health/Lifestyle/Other</u>: illegal drug use, alcohol abuse, tobacco use, among others.

According to Dr. Charles Lindemann of Oakland University, the average human ejaculation contains *180 million sperm*; some contain up to 400 million.[21] Although a male's sperm count may be lowered due to any of the aforementioned conditions, we are talking about *hundreds of millions* of sperm in one single ejaculation. Even if the average count of 180 million is cut in half, in the words of Dr. Lindemann, "all it takes is one." Thus, your mate's medications, exposure to radiation, soaking in a hot tub, or drug or alcohol abuse will *not* protect you from pregnancy.

When all is said and done, we are all human beings. The human condition is one that encompasses impulsive behavior that leads to unintended outcomes. We get caught up in passion, we are influenced by a host of factors, and an unplanned pregnancy occurs. All one can do is arm oneself with knowledge, try to make the best decisions based on that knowledge, and deal with whatever results come about as a result of those decisions.

For parents of adolescents, it is imperative to start the conversation and leave the door ajar for future "mythbusting" discussions. Keeping judgment and assumptions at bay, while educating and embracing the realities of life's decisions, will encourage the avenues of communication to flow in both directions. Don't make like an ostrich; get out there and talk! Read a book with your child about sexual health, sit down with your child at the computer and explore websites listed in this chapter. You can do it!

"Nobody ever did, or ever will, escape the consequences of his or her choices."
Alfred A. Montapert, author/philosopher

Chapter 14: Contemplating Motherhood

Most people spend ample time in contemplation before entering into marriage. In the Catholic religion, couples must go through full-day marriage preparation classes (called PreCana) that deal with topics such as communication, expectations, intimacy, and natural family planning. Wouldn't it be nice if a class was widely available to couples to help them with the contemplation of having a child?

In this book, I consistently refer to the effect of children on their moms and vice versa. Some of what I've written can also be applied to men; however, as discussed in Chapter 7, men are not grilled as regularly about procreation, perhaps because their biological clocks seem infinite, as displayed by late-in-life fathers such as Steve Martin (fathering his first child at 67) and Julio Iglesias, Sr. (siring a child at age 89 and one more born posthumously). Men's childbearing years span the bulk of their lives, whereas women's optimal childbearing years are confined to a much narrower timeframe, coinciding with their years of advanced education and career formation.

The list of women who should have never become mothers is heartbreaking. Think of the portrayal of Joan Crawford as *Mommy Dearest*. Or Susan Smith of South Carolina and the 1994 filicide of her two little boys; strapping her toddler sons into their car seats before rolling them into a lake to death by drowning and then claiming she'd been the victim of a carjacking and her sons had been kidnapped. All this, reportedly, so that she could be free to resume an affair with a local man. Perhaps Ms. Smith had heard of the case of Diane Downs from 11 years earlier, with eerily similar details (getting rid of her children so she could resume an affair). Downs drove her three children to a rural road in Oregon and shot all three, after which she claimed to have been carjacked by a strange man who shot her children (one died; two survived).

On the less drastic side is the narcissistic mother who consistently puts her own needs ahead of her child's. We've all seen or heard of these women. The mother who manipulates her child for her own goals; or cares more about her child's looks or accomplishments than the child's feelings. According to Dr. Karyl McBride, there are six categories of maternal narcissism: [1]

- the "flamboyant-extrovert" (loved by the masses but feared by her children who know that what matters most is how they make her appear to the world);
- the "accomplishment-oriented" (success depends upon what you do, not who you are; if you fail to meet her expectations, she responds with fury);
- the "psychosomatic" (uses illnesses and aches to manipulate others; you cannot be sicker than her because she'll up the ante);
- the "addicted" (bottle or drug comes before the child);
- the "secretly mean" (the mother who is loving in public but cruel at home);
- the "emotionally needy" (while all narcissistic moms fit this category, this mother shows the characteristic more openly than the others).

Having any one of these kinds of narcissistic mothers can amount to a childhood without proper nurturing where barriers stand in the way of empathy. According to Dr. McBride, there are alarming effects on children raised by narcissistic mothers. They grow up never feeling quite good enough, questioning whether they are lovable, and they don't trust their own feelings.

As discussed throughout this book, parenthood is challenging, exhausting, costly, and irreversible. We would do well to be open to alternative paths for today's generation, and encourage young adults to ponder whether parenthood is the path they should pursue. Below are a few questions for "parental prospects" to consider:

- What are your motivations for having a child? E.g., creating an heir, carrying on the family name, or making a partner happy. If the goal is carrying on the family name (Which name? Yours or your partner's?)
- How much of your desire for a child is biologically driven? E.g., biological clock running down, replicating one's DNA.
- Is your desire for a child impacted by the expectations of family or friends?
- How much of your desire for a child is socially motivated? E.g., a child as an outward sign of success; the feeling of being needed; wanting to fit in with one's peers.
- Do you think having kids is a kind of insurance in your old age? E.g., insurance against later regret or someone to care for you when you're elderly.
- Would your own parent be judgmental or hurt if you decided *not* to have children?
- Do you feel your friends and family would be supportive of your decision, whatever that may be?
- How do you define "good opportunities" for a child? Do you feel that your situation would afford a child good opportunities?
- Can you afford a child without significant help from external sources?

- How will your career be affected? Is frequent travel and/or overtime required?
- Who will watch your child when you work? Who will watch your child when he is ill and you have to work (frequent in the early years)? Who will watch your child when *you* are sick?
- If you are contemplating single motherhood, do you have someone to help you with the consequences of this choice? (Parenting Partner) Have you discussed your needs with that person(s)?
- Last but not least, are you concerned about the accelerated rate of extinction of species beyond the natural rate that is attributed to overpopulation of our planet? There's a saying among ecologists: No rain drop feels it is responsible for the flood. Demographers suggest that the "replacement fertility rate" of 2.1 children per woman will stabilize world population; higher rates increase world population.

Following are possible life scenarios to contemplate:
  A. Solo; no kids—this might include religious endeavors or the eternal bachelorette.
  B. Marriage/cohabitation; no kids—includes same-sex unions.
  C. Marriage/cohabitation; with kid(s)—includes same-sex unions.
  D. Solo; with kid(s).

Ask yourself what you want out of life. You cannot have it all. Sorry, you just can't. Anyone who leads you to believe you can is wrong. Life is about choices. One choice may naturally preclude another. For example, choosing options C or D above will naturally preclude the conditions present in A and B. Also, since not all relationships withstand the stress of children, going from B to C may end up bumping you to D.

Contemplation of motherhood is a serious matter; a decision that will permanently alter the landscape of your life (and those closest to you), as well as set the life stage for a child. Observe and talk to women with kids. Find out how they really feel about the decisions they've made. Ask them what they may have done differently. You may find that they wish they had furthered their education before having kids. Or that they would have put off motherhood for a few more years until they'd had a chance to save for a down payment on a home. I can almost guarantee you they won't tell you that they wish they hadn't pursued motherhood; for to do so would erase a child whom they love. Then assess the answers in light of your own circumstances.

If possible, explore this topic with your own mother (perhaps give your mom a copy of this book to set the stage). Mothers know how hard it is to do what they do. But they usually don't talk about their internal struggles with their kids. They do not talk about the paths that were *not* chosen that would have led them elsewhere, because to do this might imply a hint of regret. Perhaps mothers don't think their children will understand the difference between regret and recognition of the path not taken. In addition, in talking openly about this topic, perhaps moms are afraid of hearing a hint of regret from their children for decisions that were made on their behalf.

But if these discussions never happen, how can the next generation learn from history? Bringing these topics out of the family closet and into the light of day just might clear out a whole bunch of junk we knew was hidden but didn't want to deal with.

Equally important would be to speak with women who are living their lives without motherhood; voices which you will read in the next chapter. Study their examples and

126

consider how similar your inner self may be to one of them. There are plenty of women who do not want motherhood. If you are one, take heart that you are not alone.

No one ever said contemplating motherhood would be easy. But a woman can arm herself with reality-based knowledge before making decisions that will impact the rest of her life. To thine own self be true—and disregard the rest.

"Two roads diverged in a wood, and I,
I took the one less traveled by..."
Robert Frost, poet

Chapter 15: The Other Side of Motherhood

Women without children exist in significant numbers in the United States and many countries around the world. Striving to use the correct words to describe these women, I consulted an on-line dictionary, which listed only one antonym for "mother"—the word "father."[1] There are other words that might serve as an antonym for mother, such as "nullipara" (a woman who has never borne a child); however, that word doesn't fit for a woman who bore a child and then gave the child up for adoption. She's not a mother, nor is she nulliparous.

Many women who are not mothers prefer the term "childfree" (CF) to "childless," since the former has a connotation of power, versus the latter which has a connotation of being "less than." This is a matter of semantics; if one closely examines the feelings attached to one word choice over the other, the dynamics of these adjectives become clearer. I encourage you to seek to understand, rather than judge.

The idea that women may not want motherhood is unsettling for many people, and these uneasy people communicate their discord, often loudly. From economists (who condemn CF people for not producing future consumers and taxpayers)—to journalists (who view a female's writing skill as limited if she is not a mother, as happened with Maeve Binchy)—to one's peers in the workplace and the community—too often, the life choices or circumstances of females' lives are held up for display for others to act as judge and jury. If a woman does not have children, then the jury searches for her alibi before exoneration (in the form of pity for the infertile or justification for those who commit their lives to lofty goals/causes) before sentencing her to a lifetime of guilt (deeming her lacking, selfish or dysfunctional).

Many CF women disagree with the idea that they must live their lives in a certain manner in order to justify their existence. Quite literally, CF women are bone-tired of defending themselves from those who question them in ways that make them feel that they owe the world an explanation for how they live their lives. There are numerous books, articles, and blogs designed to justify or demystify being childless, childfree or "without child," written mainly by women who are, themselves, not mothers. Some want to get their voices out there in hopes that people will stop pestering them with intrusive questions; others just want to set the record straight on the circumstances or choices that led to the lives they are leading; and some just want to be left the hell alone, to live their lives in peace.

The media is full of "mommy war" stories, describing conflicts between warring factions of mothers on topics from breastfed versus formula-fed, to foregoing paid employment versus working outside the home, to attachment-parenting versus other child-rearing methods. Gathering steam is another type of war, largely fueled by women, a sort of "unmommy war," if you will, and it has the potential to fracture the inner selves of childless women due to decisions or circumstances within or outside of their control. Caustic, judgmental comments are hurled across the demarcation line, leaving hurt feelings in their wake.

After Calista[*] (introduced in Chapter 6) learned that I am a mom who believes in the right of my daughter and every woman to decide whether motherhood is the right path, she sighed, "I'm so glad there are people like you on our side." This reaction was unsettling. Calista's statement haunts me because I envision my daughter expressing it someday, or one of my five beautiful great-nieces. It breaks my heart to think of women who feel that the world is against them based on one aspect of their lives—because they are not mothers.

In a wonderful show of compassion and support between women, in honor of August 2013 as National Breastfeeding Awareness Month, author and blogger Suzanne Barston spearheaded a social media campaign designed to tear down the barriers separating women who breastfeed their babies from those who formula-feed.[2] In a picture posted on the Internet, we see a woman with her baby, and she's holding a sign that says, "I Support You." The world would be a warmer place if it were filled with women holding signs of support for each other.

Although the core value of family is one that is shared around the world, its definition varies. For most, the definition of family begins with one's own parents; biological parents, adoptive parents, stepparents, or foster parents. As children grow into adulthood, their definition of family changes.

Author Barbara Graham eloquently describes this evolution as a series of concentric circles, like the rings of a tree, with each of us stationed at the center of our own innermost ring.[3] Those in the innermost circle are the people dearest to us; our core people are those closest to us in the literal or figurative sense. In each succeeding ring are other people in our lives. Although parents belong in a child's innermost circle when the child is young, they don't

---

* Name has been changed.

necessarily stay there; often, parents drop back a ring or two in their children's lives, especially when their children start their own families—whatever that family looks like. There are "families of two" (a couple); there are families-of-choice consisting of the friends we let into our lives; pet-owners consider their pets part of their family. Gay marriage is not legal in all of the states, but it constitutes the definition of family by those who believe in it. The point is, there is not a universal definition of family, and one definition should not diminish another. Just because you don't have children doesn't mean you miss out on family.

In the African American culture, opposition to motherhood as a strategy of resistance began during the slavery era when more babies meant more slaves; a time when babies were ripped from their mothers' arms. In a melding of the personal and the political, there are African American women today who reject motherhood rather than raise a child in a culture that discriminates on the basis of ethnicity, class, gender, etc. According to Joyce Meier of the University of Michigan, "the refusal of motherhood by African American women shows how historical oppression recurs in the present, and how the black woman's body continues to be the site of both domination and resistance."[4]

Patricia Hill Collins, Professor of Sociology at the University of Maryland, esteemed social theorist, and a prolific author on the topic of black feminism, describes the practice of "othermothering," which developed from West African tradition with collective systems of "mothering networks."[5] According to Collins, "The West African tradition of othermothering was retained by enslaved African Americans out of necessity. Slavery gave rise to a distinct tradition of African American motherhood in which the custom of othermothering was emphasized and

131

elaborated." Especially as mothers were separated from their children against their will.

Author Elizabeth Gilbert writes on the topic of othermothering. Something she calls the "Auntie Brigade," made up of childless aunts who, throughout history, have othermothered their nieces or nephews.[6] Gilbert highlighted the lives of Leo Tolstoy, Truman Capote, and the Brontë sisters, all of whom were raised by their childless aunts. John Lennon was also raised by his aunt, who encouraged him to become an artist. And Frank Lloyd Wright's first building was commissioned by his two childless aunts. More examples of othermothering can be found in the interviews presented in this chapter.

Seventy women without children were interviewed or surveyed for this book, mainly from the United States, plus a handful of international women. The women come from all walks of life; they are of varying ages, ethnicities, religions, educational levels, and income brackets. There are college students, high-level managers, hair dressers, authors, doctors, graphic designers, scientists, secretaries, teachers, as well as retirees and the temporarily-unemployed; the list goes on. The vast majority of these women grew up assuming they would become moms someday because of messages they heard growing up, examples they observed, or visceral visions they had for their futures. The majority of these women have struggled with assumptions held for them by others. Many bristle when they hear assumptions about how their lives are supposed to look. Others have quietly come to terms with how their lives have played out. Too many are still navigating the minefield of assumptions.

This chapter is devoted to all the women who were so generous with their time and honesty. By sharing the flip side of the motherhood coin, I hope to enlarge the vision that we all hold for women who are not mothers. For each comment, please remember that there are countless women who hold similar sentiments.

Christine Walker, spouse of Robert Walker (President of the Population Institute), described how she came to live her life without motherhood. Christine did a lot of babysitting in her high school days, and one experience stands out in her mind. Babysitting for a neighbor who was in the hospital having her fourth child, Christine cared for twin 3-year-old boys and a 5-year-old girl for three days; and she found that she didn't like the noise, crying, and clean-up involved. According to Christine, "That finished me off." She met her husband in college and found that neither was interested in having kids. After nearly four decades of marriage, the Walkers are very close. And they have "never looked back"—they have never regretted their decision not to have kids.

Cheryl* comes from working class Polish immigrants, and African American grandparents from the south whose education stopped at eighth grade. For this reason, Cheryl is especially proud of her master's degree. She said, "When I graduated, I felt so proud…proud for my family." When Cheryl was 16, she heard the comment that being a mother is the quintessential female experience, and remembers feeling in her gut that there was something wrong with that statement. Until Cheryl was 25, she had assumed she would be a mom someday; however, after a lot of soul searching, she realized that opting out of motherhood was an option for her life. In her late 20s, Cheryl works as an early childhood educator, "I see the consequences of what happens when you have a child when you're not prepared, with all the stressors." She says, "A lot of times I don't volunteer that I don't want kids." She

---

* Name has been changed

doesn't want to hear responses that hint that she doesn't know what she wants (e.g., "you'll change your mind" or "you have time"). She also doesn't like comments such as, "You should have kids so you can leave a legacy."

The hardest comments for Cheryl to digest are ones that come from those closest to her. Once Cheryl made up her mind not to have kids, she told her mother. "My mom used to drop hints all the time and then glare at me; but she's beginning to accept that I won't give her grandkids...now she comments about my siblings who will be 'the ones' to give her grandkids." Cheryl is passionate about her work with underprivileged kids. "I've always wanted to work where I'd have the most impact...low income kids need great teachers." Having left the Catholic church once she realized she didn't want to have children, Cheryl still refers to her religious background as having instilled in her an ethic of serving others; and she asks herself how she can use her talents to help other people. Her words, "I want to be a hero," pretty much sum it up.

As a child, Alice* was bombarded by female stereotypes. Carrying around her baby doll by the foot, she was counseled on how to properly "care" for it; but she preferred running science experiments on it instead. As a young teen, Alice became depressed when people around her said that she would have babies one day. Finally, her mom told her that it was okay to be the person she was meant to be and make her own decisions. Alice said, "I am so grateful for that permission," and that her mother's prescient response "allowed me to open the door to becoming the content, fun-loving childfree woman I am today." As it turns out, Alice's early love of science paid off. Entering the world of medicine, she once made a treatment suggestion that resulted in the saving of a

---

* Names have been changed.

patient's life on the operating room table. Seeing that patient's smile in the recovery room is just one moment out of many when Alice knows she is living the life she is meant to live. She and her husband share a full, loving, happy life—without regrets—and without children.

Some women are drawn more to a specific goal than to motherhood. As a young adolescent, Cathy* remembers driving with her dad and voicing her dream of owning her own business someday. Her dad's words resonate with her to this day, "You can do whatever you set your mind to!" Cathy is grateful that her parents have been supportive of her choices and that there was no assumption that motherhood needed to be a part of the equation. Not surprisingly, Cathy is an entrepreneur with her own business. She is in her mid-40s, single, has never had kids, and lives a full, happy life. Her gratitude overflows for her open-minded parents and their support.

Unfortunately, Robin* did not experience the support that Cathy did. She said, "I don't think anyone in my immediate sphere ever thought of parenthood as a choice." This filled Robin with dread because she has never felt drawn to motherhood. Being told by family members that she would never find a partner who would stay with her if she didn't want kids also contributed to Robin's unease. Robin went on to find a loving partner who is committed to sharing a "childfree" lifestyle. She said, "Treating parenthood like an inevitability can ruin lives for people like me."

Audrey* was married young but the time never seemed right for kids. Divorced for many years, Audrey is in her late 40s and feels strongly that a child is not necessary to a fulfilled life: "Self-fulfillment does not come from an

---

* Names have been changed

outside source such as a child or husband...fulfillment comes from inside." Although Audrey never felt a strong itch for motherhood, she had considered adoption at one time. She is adamant that replicating her DNA was never important to her; that there is too much need out there. As a hairdresser, she sometimes feels like a "therapist to the world." She feels good that she can lend an ear; she's even given advice to battered women in the past. Talking with Audrey, one gets the sense that not much gets past her, that she is a very good listener.

Audrey relishes the small things in life such as spending time with family and friends. She spoke of her relief when her sister had a baby; her compassion was for her mom, to experience being a grandmother. Audrey also enjoys traveling to out-of-the-way places such as kayaking in Canada or glacier trekking in Alaska, experiences that garner awe. When we spoke, Audrey had just lost her dog, whom she loved with an unconditional heart. Audrey possesses a heart big enough for all creatures—big and small—in the big city where she lives and in nature.

Introduced in Chapter 13, Sascha* had a poster mom for supportive discussions about the realities of sexual health and motherhood. When Sascha was in her 30s and experienced medical issues that led to a hysterectomy at 40, her mother's past support helped Sascha to make peace with her situation despite having assumed she would have a child someday. If not for her mom's open-minded discourse, Sascha may well have spiraled into despair as other women have done when faced with the dissipation of a lifelong assumption. Sascha thrives on busy, "I feel like there's always so much to do...public service is very important to me, giving back to the community, mentoring, doing food drives. I ask my friends how they do all that I

---

* Names have been changed.

136

do and raise kids too." Reflecting on Maslow's description of "peak experiences," Sascha talked about her trip to visit an aunt in Germany. "Getting to see Europe, I saw castles, drove through the Alps and Milan; it was thrilling to see the world outside of the U.S." Growing up, she did not have a close relationship with her African American father's family (her dad died when Sascha was 8); thus, visiting extended family was especially meaningful.

Colleen* can envision herself 20 years from now with or without a child of her own. In her early 30s, she used to think she could do the single-mom thing but she has changed her mind, "I couldn't do it alone, financially or emotionally." Colleen said that the idea of foregoing motherhood used to bother her but she's making peace with it as she gets older. "Getting to this age, seeing my friends in crappy marriages, people tell me all the time how tiring it is to have kids…it makes me not want to do it." Colleen has found "a million things" that make her happy and so much to do with her time. She said, "I've worked hard to get where I am; I'm independent, I have plans to buy a condo and travel." To the cliché "the grass is always greener on the other side," Colleen quipped, "My side is really green and plush!"

Helen* laughed when she heard, "You must have had a horrible childhood," because she describes her parents as "Ozzie and Harriett." She said, "The decision not to pursue motherhood came down to the standard for parenting my mom and dad set; I knew I didn't have the resources to be the kind of mother I wanted to be. To me, it would have been selfish to pursue motherhood despite the lack of time and resources." In her mid-60s, Helen realized from a young age that she enjoyed her freedom. She is comfortable with herself and her life of peace and solitude.

* Names have been changed

137

Helen heard her friends say, "poor Helen," while they were marrying and having kids; 20 years later, it was "lucky Helen," when several of them were getting divorced and dealing with the aftermath. Helen has heard hints that she might be gay. She's active in promoting gay rights, so perhaps this is an understandable jump for someone to make. But she's not gay. Nor does she hold any regret about not getting married or having children. And she's not lonely: "A perfect night out is dinner and a play, and I have friends who do that with me."

Olivia* (introduced in Chapter 6) had a tumultuous childhood. I don't offer this information as a way of categorizing Olivia, but as a way of setting the context for the prayer that she utters each night, "I lay in bed and thank God for the peace in my life." I specifically chose the alias "Olivia" because its meaning is peace (i.e., the olive branch). Olivia was married at one time, got divorced, and with the passing of time, so too went the idea of becoming a mom. She loves being with friends, but says her favorite place in the world is at home in her own peaceful environment.

A black Roman Catholic, Jetta* grew up assuming she'd have kids. She said, "The realization hit me that I didn't want to have kids when I was working at a daycare center one summer and I spent the whole time feeling frustrated." Now in her late 20s, Jetta's friends hound her about her decision not to have children, remarking that they thought she'd have changed her mind by now. The same friends who call Jetta to complain about their kids and their hectic lives ask her, almost in the same breath, "*Why* don't you want to be a mommy?"

---

* Names have been changed.

Whether a woman expressed her disinterest in motherhood, or whether it just never happened for her (through circumstance or biology), every woman I spoke with has experienced some sort of intrusive question, comment, or assumption. One woman was asked, "Why don't you become a nun?" Another was advised to lie, to tell people she "can't have kids;" but she doesn't want to lie in order to protect herself from the judgment of others. Some women have developed clever quips as they've grown tired of overly inquisitive people who trespass into private areas of their lives. Such as, "I like dogs but I don't want one; I like kids but I don't want one." Others say nothing at all; they just turn away from those who are overly inquisitive. One woman talked of how she used to receive a lot of pressure from family and friends, so she got new friends and disassociated with family. Next time you are tempted to ask an intrusive question of a woman without children, imagine the sentiment that might be drifting quietly in the back of her mind.

Countless women who are not mothers throw their energy into volunteer work and other lofty endeavors. The following examples are *not* meant to *justify* the lifestyles of these women, but as a way of exhibiting the "collective energy" of women who are not busy chasing after their own brood.

One nonmom was named Humanitarian of the Year by her peers in a statewide professional organization. Another woman volunteers her time as a photographer at animal adoption centers and feels a thrill when someone comments that her picture brought them in to see an animal. Others have raised tens of thousands of dollars for disaster relief, devoted their holidays to work in soup kitchens, served as mentors to underprivileged youth, and have volunteered hundreds of hours sewing "memory bears for hospice" (a meaningful symbol of a recently-deceased loved one).

There are many women without children who serve as examples for today's females who are evaluating various life choices. Following are some noteworthy nonmothers who have impacted society in innumerable ways: Helen Keller (world-renown activist for people with disabilities, suffragist, author, lecturer), Amelia Earhart (first female aviator to fly solo across the Atlantic); Susan B. Anthony (played pivotal role in women's suffrage); Gloria Steinem (women's rights advocate); Sally Ride (first female astronaut); Condoleezza Rice (first female African American U.S. Secretary of State); Frida Kahlo (one of the most talented painters of the 20th century); Eva Peron (First Lady of Argentina, advocate for women's suffrage and the lives of the poor); Jane Addams (whose work on behalf of women, children, and immigrants led to immeasurable social reform).

Rosa Parks was the "Mother of the Civil Rights Movement," yet Ms. Parks was not a mother. With grandparents who were slaves, Ms. Parks grew up with a very personal awareness of the inequities of life. After Ms. Parks's 1955 arrest for not giving up her seat on a bus in Montgomery, Alabama, she devoted the remainder of her life to civil rights causes.

The author of *Silent Spring*, Rachel Carson researched the harmful effects of toxic chemicals on the earth's ecosystem and on human life. Carson wrote how cancer in children went from a medical rarity to the most common disease causing death. Two hundred chemicals were created between the mid-1940s and 1962; for farms, gardens, forests, and homes. Carson's book caused a public outcry that led to the eventual banning of DDT (a pesticide and carcinogen) in 1972 and the passing of the Endangered Species Act in 1973.

Stephanie Mills was catapulted to notoriety when, in her 1969 college commencement address, she declared, "I am terribly saddened by the fact that the most humane thing for me to do is to have no children at all."[7] Mills explained, "I asked myself what kind of world my children would grow up in. And the answer was, 'not very pretty, not very clean.' Because if population continues to grow, the facilities to accommodate that population must grow too. Thus we have more highways and fewer trees, more electricity… more cities and less clean air." Mills is a renowned lecturer on ecological restoration and a Fellow of the Post Carbon Institute (think-tank for 21st century global sustainability issues).

In the category of writers, to name just a few, there are: Jane Austen, Emily Brontë, Virginia Woolf, Emily Dickinson, Maeve Binchy, Elizabeth Gilbert, and Julia Child (author and chef).

A sampling of actors who have never had children and/or have made statements that they enjoy their lives without children include: Betty White, Katharine Hepburn, Ann-Margret, Dana Delany, Ashley Judd, Kathy Bates, Cameron Diaz, Renee Zellweger, Angelica Huston, Bo Derek, Linda Evans, and Lily Tomlin.

All of the aforementioned women lived or are living lives without motherhood. They pursued lives of science, politics, and/or various forms of artistry/craft. Can anyone rightfully say that any of these women's lives lacked meaning? Were they (or are they) selfish or foolish women who chose paths less happy or fulfilled than those women who opted for motherhood? And for every name mentioned, can you imagine 100 (or 500 or 1,000) other women who would have liked to follow paths such as these women even if it meant opting out of motherhood? I don't mean choosing a life of fame and fortune; rather, pursuing

141

their passions, honing their craft, and finding their own paths to an authentic life.

There are many paths women travel that do not lead them to motherhood. Some consciously choose the road less traveled. Others find that the twists and turns their lives have taken led them down other paths. Those who have the hardest time finding peace are those who do not hear acceptance for who they are or where they're headed. Some women speak of acceptance from their parents as "permission" to pursue something other than motherhood. The word "permission" implies a mandate. Is this how women should view such a personal, life-altering decision?

Unless one has walked in the shoes of every woman who is *not* a mother, one cannot fully appreciate her journey. We need to listen with open minds and open hearts to these women; they are our daughters, nieces, best friends; they are today's generation of women who will pave the way for the next generation.

"My fullest concentration of energy is available to me
only when I integrate all the parts of me…without the
restriction of externally imposed definition."
Audre Lorde, poet/lecturer

Chapter 16: Voices of the Twelve Percent

In a poll I conducted with 100+ women who are mothers of
daughters (from across the U.S.), 88% responded that they
assume their daughters will become mothers someday.
This leaves 12% who do *not* hold this assumption.

When a mother thinks about her daughter following in her
footsteps by becoming a mom herself, this can feel like
validation of the mother's own lifestyle. Moms fiercely
love their kids and many believe that their daughters will
want to experience what they experienced. When
daughters do not want motherhood, this can become a
source of contention or confusion.

The talk show, *The View,* featured journalist Barbara
Walters speaking up for her daughter who does not want to
have kids. According to Ms. Walters, her daughter receives
looks from people who think there's something wrong with
her when she voices disinterest in motherhood. Co-host
Sherri Shepherd gushed about her young son and how the
wonder of having kids doesn't compare to anything else.
To which Ms. Walters responded, "Not everyone wants
that."

The premise of *The View* has been for five women to
discuss "hot topics," and controversy is expected. As a
celebrity, Walters has an easier time speaking up for her
daughter's choice to opt out of motherhood. But what
about the average mother on the street? Does the average
mom feel comfortable expressing that her daughter "is who

she is" if she doesn't want motherhood? Or does she offer justification for her daughter's choices, listing all her accomplishments as a way of explaining and defending her status?

Fortunately, there are moms who are adamant about letting their daughters choose their own path. Journalist Suzanne Moore wrote about her three daughters, "People often ask me if I look forward to becoming a grandmother. With my two eldest in their 20s, it's a fair enough question, but how to answer it?…Fundamentally, this one is not about me. It's about the choices my daughters have and what circumstances they find themselves in…Having kids gives meaning to lives, but this is not the only way to have a meaningful and wonderful life...Whether we call this childless or childfree depends on a whole set of narratives that are procreating rapidly but are really divisive attempts to isolate women instead of uniting us…I hope my own children feel supported whatever they decide."[1]

Playwright Catherine Johnson may be best known for her script for the musical *Mamma Mia* and the screenplay for the movie of the same name. In an exclusive interview, Catherine told me, "I don't make any assumptions as far as my daughter is concerned! I would be fine if she opts out of motherhood; I support her choice whatever it is." When I asked her about talking with her daughter about motherhood, Catherine replied, "I would talk about my own experience of motherhood *only if she asked me to*. I can't imagine putting any pressure on her. I truly do *not* believe she would be 'missing out' if she doesn't have children and I certainly don't mind if I'm never a grandmother. This isn't because I haven't personally felt extraordinarily fulfilled as a mother. I love my children more than anything and I know they've made my world remarkably richer. But that was my choice and I would honor and respect my daughter's choice if it was different."

144

Lauri Burns is a technology executive at a Fortune 100 company, published author, and Founder of The Teen Project. Over the past two decades, Lauri has taken in many of Orange County's (Los Angeles area) toughest girls, having invited her 18th foster child into her personal home by 2006. When I spoke with Lauri, she discussed her biological daughter and her many foster daughters, "Speaking as someone who has raised 30 foster kids—with emancipated kids, the number is closer to 60—I know for sure that instilling expectations with regard to motherhood would be emotionally unhealthy." Lauri has been called "The Teen Whisperer" because of her talent for communicating with teens and her ability to see the big picture. Referring to her 31-year-old biological daughter, Lauri said, "I would be fine if she did not become a mother…she works with kids with autism and she has already said to me, 'I'm working with all these kids, how can I have my own?'"

Some mothers I polled reflected on their own pre-motherhood experiences. Annette* remembers being pressured by her mom and vows never to do this to her own daughter. Jane* responded, "No matter how successful I was in my career, all people seemed to ask about was when I would get married and have kids…always hinting at my biological clock." Jane has two teenage daughters, and she does not like to think of them being hounded. Linda* said, "I absolutely would *not* communicate any expectation to my daughter; with all the situations where people struggle to have a baby, I wouldn't want to add pressure…if my daughter and her husband have a baby, great; if not, that's good too as long as they're happy."

Danielle* has three kids, two daughters and a son. She said that she used to harbor an assumption that both her

---

* Names have been changed.

daughters would have children someday. When her oldest daughter got married, she and her husband asked for Danielle's opinion on having just one child. Danielle responded that it was none of her business and whatever decision they made was entirely up to them. When Danielle's second oldest daughter was 15, she announced that she was never having kids; she never asked for her mom's opinion and Danielle never offered one. Now pushing 30, this same daughter still says she'll never have a child; and Danielle still doesn't offer any opinions. "My children are the light of my life…but I believe beyond a shadow of a doubt that motherhood is too deep of a personal choice to meddle in."

The mother of two daughters, Jeanette* spoke about the importance of respecting her two daughters' individuality, "Motherhood is my journey, not theirs." Lena* echoed Jeanette's thoughts about *not* projecting her own feelings about motherhood onto her daughter, "Nothing is as difficult or wonderful as motherhood; but motherhood comes at a great cost and is a deep sacrifice. There is a person my daughter may become if she does *not* choose to become a mother, and I am interested in knowing that person. On the other hand, there is a person she could become if she decides to become a mother, and I would like to know that person as well. In any case, I hope the choice is all hers; she will choose which person she becomes." Lena continued, "I can't imagine that the expression of disappointment would be welcome to the ears, or the heart, of any woman who has made the choice not to become a mother, as with any other life choice. It would not be my place to express disappointment. My job as her mother is to help her know her own heart, and to give her respite no matter her choices."

---

* Names have been changed.

It is probable that most, if not all, mothers harbor a secret hope of becoming a grandmother someday. After years of time and energy invested in our child, a grandchild seems like a just reward. Having this desire is understandable. It's what moms do with it that matters. Jen* expressed, "I have a daughter in her mid-30s who has been in a relationship for a year; I was happy that it looked serious but then realized that was a selfish 'I-want-to-be-a-grandma' thought, and that she has to walk her own path and live her own life...It would be very wrong for me to get involved in that decision."

There are no guarantees in life. If our children feel that they are letting us down if they don't want to have their own child...or if they are *unable* to fulfill their "mother's dream" of becoming a grandmother, how does that affect their inner worlds? Their self esteem? Their happiness?

Sometimes, the badgering can explode in a parent's face. As with April,* a college student who reached her point of tolerance, "My parents assume I will get married; there have been comments from them and I blew up because they wouldn't leave me alone...I went from dislike of marriage and children to complete hate for the moment."

Nicole* put it bluntly, "I am raising my daughter to make her own choices; to think that women's lives may be incomplete because they don't have children is myopic. As for becoming a grandmother, it would be selfish for me to expect my daughter to make me a grandma someday."

These are the voices of the 12% of mothers who do *not* hold the assumption that their daughters will become moms. The voices are out there, though mostly muted. We

---

* Names have been changed.

need more of these voices, with updated scripts for today's 21st century females.

"How would your life be different if you stopped making negative assumptions about people you encounter?
Let that day be today...respect their journey!"
Dr. Steve Maraboli, behavioral science academic

Chapter 17: Re-Writing the Scripts

We are all opinionated and live inside our own heads to some extent. How we react when others challenge our way of thinking or living is one of life's biggest challenges. Passion, by its virtue, is something that inspires great emotion. Passion for one's family, human dignity, religion, politics, and economic realities—all these topics can rally us to support causes we believe in. And they can also serve to divide us if we let it.

Sociologist C. Wright Mills wrote about the "sociological imagination" that urges us to think sociologically about the world, and to realize that what we think of as personal problems are widely shared by others like ourselves. Issues that seem personal are actually part of the public landscape or social structure. When a woman without children is viewed harshly, is this her own personal issue to deal with? Or do we, as a society, push for an evolution of thought that protects her? Likewise, for women who are mothers, when society attaches labels of "good mom" or "bad mom" to them, is this a personal matter for each woman to reconcile or does it reflect a larger societal issue?

According to D. Lynn O'Brien Hallstein, "Each label dismantles choices one brick at a time."[1] In her research, Hallstein traces the "mom labels" as they developed, revealing that these labels (e.g., supermom, soccer mom, alpha mom, etc.) "have played and continue to play a key role in systematically stripping the politics of choice in the service of reinscribing mothering as the most important part

149

of femininity…and equally important, the relationship between intensive mothering and contemporary feminism which continues to evolve in problematic and deeply troubling ways."

The concept of feminism evokes passion, good and bad. Accurately defined, feminism is the belief that women and men deserve equal rights and opportunities—politically, socially, and economically. In the 1960s, radical actions were required to bring about real change for women; thus, the word "feminism" absorbed negative connotations. In addition, since the feminist movement of the 1960s largely ignored non-white women, this added to the negative feel for the word. The idea of being a feminist has evolved over time, with many females stepping away from the label.

As black women have strived to develop their own scripts, author and activist Rebecca Walker wrote, "Whether young women who refuse the feminist label realize it or not, on some level they recognize that an ideal woman born of prevalent notions of how empowered women look, act, or think, is simply another impossible contrivance of perfect womanhood, another scripted role to perform in the name of biology and virtue." Walker coined the phrase "Third Wave Feminism" in her essay for Ms. Magazine in 1992, challenging a universal definition of "femininity," and incorporating the voices of women who were left out of the second wave feminist movement—young, lesbian, and/or nonwhite women.

Women come in all shapes, sizes, and with varying amounts of melanin in their skin. Their experiences, ethnicities, and sexual orientation may be different. Their goals and affinities may be different. They look at the world through different eyes. They have the right to be who they are meant to be, and pursue the goals they hold dear. Attempting to view all women through one lens is like trying to view the stars with a pair of opera glasses. You cannot see the beauty beyond your limited view.

No matter their choices, women may inevitably be called selfish. Some believe that having a child is rooted in selfish motives. Others believe the opposite, that refraining from having children reflects selfishness. The literal definition of the word selfish is: the lack of consideration for others or concerned with one's own pleasure or profit. From this definition, one could hurl this word at 99% of the free world. I experience lack of consideration when driving in my car almost every day, who doesn't? As far as being concerned with one's own profit, since money is what pays the bills, I'm not sure who among us doesn't fit into this category. And "concern with pleasure"…seriously? The pursuit of pleasure in some form is a part of the human condition. Unless one lives one's life as Mother Teresa of Calcutta did, how can anyone hurl stones from inside their pleasure-seeking glass houses?

Perhaps the poet Oscar Wilde said it best, "Selfishness is not living as one wishes to live; it is asking others to live as one wishes to live. And unselfishness is letting other people's lives alone, not interfering with them."

In a graphic display of what can happen when parents interfere too avidly in their children's lives, I read the following quote on a blog for the childfree: "I've had a lifetime of my mother dictating to me how my life should be run…I told her some truths…and she doesn't talk to me anymore but I am free of the criticism." The people who post to these kinds of blogs speak of divisiveness between themselves and those who are supposed to love them, accept them, support them. Instead, they turn to anonymous blogs where they are supported by people they can reach only through keystrokes on their computers. To the previous "post," a supportive voice responded, "Your

151

mom sounds like a classic Life Scripter; marry by age X, have your first kid by age Y." Is this what any parent strives to be? A Life Scripter? As the mother of two adults, I have learned that the bulk of my mothering was in their formative years. My mothering role now must evolve into one of friendship and respect for them as individuals, as adults.

It is important to respect those who subscribe to different ideologies or come from various backgrounds. Referring to someone as dysfunctional because they don't do as we do or feel as we feel is unjust. If we think of the Iceberg Analogy, we realize that there is so much about a person that we cannot possibly know. Which person—of which ethnicity, religion, age, income level, sexual orientation, ability—gets to define normal or functional? As we embrace the diversity of those around us, we want to reflect respect in what we say and do.

Throughout this book, there have been many references to the things people say that, knowingly or unintentionally, reflect Motherhood Catechism. Specifically, in Chapters 6 and 15, you heard the voices of women who are not mothers who have been subjected to intrusive questions, comments, and unfair judgment. This chapter is devoted to re-writing some of those outdated scripts that rankle women when it comes to the deeply personal topic of motherhood. The following re-writes are suggestions for those who want to be inclusive and supportive of the women in their lives.

Marcie* asked, "My 6-year-old daughter has already said she wants to be a mommy someday; what do I do with that?" With chants on the playground such as, "First comes love, then comes marriage, then comes baby in a baby

---

* Name has been changed.

carriage!" what's a mother to say? A creative way of dealing with the mantras kids hear came from Angela, who introduced her 7 and 9-year-old daughters to a book called, "If You Lived when Women Won Their Rights,"[2] (spanning the period 620 to 1920 when women were granted the right to vote in the U.S.). This book is one of a series geared to ages 7-10 that discusses important moments in history. Angela said that when she read the book about women's rights (or the lack thereof) to her two daughters, "It created a mini-feminist roar in our house." As females grow, talking about history and giving age-appropriate doses of reality gives them new scripts and broadens the images of what their futures may hold.

THE YOUNG DAUGHTER
The following is a script analysis of the interaction between a 6-year-old and her mother: The daughter exclaims, "I want to be a mommy someday!" The mother responds, "Oh sweetheart, I just know that you'll make a great mommy someday. I can tell by the way you dote on your little cousin whenever he's around; you have wonderful mothering instincts!"

The re-write: A 6-year-old girl expresses that she wants to be a mom someday; and her mom responds, "I love being your mom; your happiness means so much to me. Whatever you choose for your life, I will be happy so long as you are happy. Did you know that in Great-Grandma Mary's day, women were not allowed to work outside the home when they were pregnant?" The daughter responds with an incredulous, "What?!" And her mom says, "That's right, at one time, women weren't even allowed to vote…say, how about we read this book (geared for young readers) on women's history together? And another day, we can jump on the Internet and read up on some women who have done some really cool stuff, such as Rosa Parks or Helen Keller. We are so lucky to live in a

153

world where strong women have come before us." The mother has not reinforced nor negated her young daughter's comments about being a mom. She simply shared a history lesson and offered to tell her the stories of some exceedingly strong women.

THE HIGH SCHOOL REUNION

A male alum encounters a woman he hasn't talked to in 20 years. A few minutes into the conversation, he asks, "How many kids do you have?" The woman, who has no children, is incredulous. She wonders why the question has to be asked at all, let alone why her ex-schoolmate skipped right over the question, "Do you have kids?" and went straight to, "How many?"

The re-write: Same two characters, and this time the male alum exclaims, "Hi! How are you? You look great! Do you still live in the area? What have you been up to the past 20 years?" They engage in a comfortable, friendly conversation where the woman is not compelled to talk about her status as a nonmom.

THE EXASPERATED MOTHER

Next, we find a mother who is exasperated that her teenage daughter who has, for what seems like the millionth time, taken her expensive make-up. Feeling that her rights are being trampled on in light of repeated requests to leave her things alone, the woman bangs on her daughter's closed, locked bedroom door. Her daughter opens the door and hands over the make-up with a look that communicates her disinterest in how her actions affect her mom. To which her mom rants, "I hope you have a daughter and she does exactly the kinds of things you do to me!" Ahh, the mother's curse.

The re-write: Same situation. Teenage daughter helping herself to things she should not. Her mother,

154

though irritated, says, "Wow, parenting teenagers is a challenging job and, quite honestly, your actions wear on my patience. Tell me, how would you respond if you had a roommate who helped herself to your make-up repeatedly? Would you feel disrespected or irritated? I'm all ears if you have a remedy for this situation."

THE CO-WORKER LUNCH
A group of female co-workers go out to lunch; a few of them are mothers, and they get on the topic of their kids. One of the mothers asks a co-worker who is not a mother when she's going to get around to having kids. The receiver of the question is caught off guard; she doesn't feel it's appropriate for people to grill her on the topic, especially when she's felt conflicted about it for years. She responds, "I don't think I'm ever going to have kids; I like kids, but I've just never felt that motherhood tug." Gasps of surprise erupt from the mothers at the table, and one says, "But aren't you afraid you'll end up with no one to care for you when you're old?" The woman being questioned feels defensive; but rather than make a scene, she offers a half-hearted answer about nursing homes being filled with people with children, while inside she is seething and resolves not to hang out with these people anymore. She understands that planning for old age begins in your 20s, she puts as much into her 401(k) account as possible, and deep down she knows that having kids is not an insurance policy for old age.

The re-write: A luncheon of female co-workers, some are mothers, some not. The topic of children come up, but the mothers at the table understand that people without kids don't necessarily enjoy tales from the motherhood playbook; so they make only the biggest announcements (e.g., Susie just made the speech team, Charlie just started pre-school), then they move on to other titillating topics, such as, the latest scoop on the new person

155

hired into the accounting department, or a movie starring some hunk actor. Everyone at the table understands that choosing topics that interest everyone is important in order for those present to feel included.

THE ASPIRING DAUGHTER
A mother hears her 12-year-old daughter exclaim, "I think I want to be a writer, that way I can be a stay-at-home mom." The mother, who has experienced life as a "stay-at-home" mom and understands how hard it can be to squeeze in time for a shower, let alone time to concentrate on an artistic endeavor, keeps her mouth shut. And she thinks to herself, "She'll find out that it's not as easy as it sounds."

The re-write: 12-year-old daughter engages in the "design process" for her life. Her mother responds with, "Sweetheart, if you have a passion for writing, I encourage you to pursue it. If your goal of being a writer is a way to design a life that includes being at home with kids, should you decide to have them, then I will share some of my own experiences from when I quit my job to care for my kids. There will be big expanses of time where you get very little time to yourself. I'm not saying it can't be done, but when you think about your future and the career you want to pursue, I want you to be armed with realistic ideas versus the romantic ones that you see in movies." The daughter accepts this information and internalizes it; filing it away for later use. Then her mom says, "Now how about I challenge you to a game of chess?" The mother has not judged her daughter's idea; she offered a dose of reality and encouraged her to think in broad terms about her future. She also challenged her daughter to a game of strategy, requiring critical thinking skills.

THE WANNABE GRANDMOTHER
A mother hangs up the phone and turns to her 29-year-old daughter. Her daughter, who has expressed her disinterest

156

in motherhood in the past, still lives at home. The mother says, "That was Aunt Lucy, she's going to be a grandma...she's so lucky!" Envy exudes from every syllable and despair shoots from the mother's eyes. The daughter, an only child, feels guilty and questions her career aspirations and non-maternal feelings. A few months later, the daughter moves out and starts ignoring her mother's phone calls and requests for visits. She's tired of feeling guilty and defending her choices. She wants to be at peace with her life.

The re-write: The mother tells her daughter about Aunt Lucy becoming a grandma. No envy or despair is apparent; just the sharing of family news. The mother, knowing her daughter's disinterest in motherhood, follows up the statement with, "By the way, have I told you lately how lucky I am to have you as my daughter? What a treat to have a daughter who is also a friend. Want to see that new play that's in town next week?" The mom has skillfully shared "baby" news without instilling guilt, reminded her daughter that she loves her for who she is, just as she is, and then changes the subject to a shared passion.

THE BRIDAL SHOWER
In a room filled with women, the bride-to-be breaks a ribbon. Someone in the room exclaims gleefully, "For every ribbon you break, that's the number of babies you're going to have! You'd better not break too many!"

The re-write: A bridal shower, the room includes the groom-to-be. The couple have already reached a private agreement that neither wants to have children. Opening of the presents begins and the bride-to-be breaks a ribbon. Not having shared their private decision not to have kids, she winces and waits for the inevitable exclamation about ribbon-breaking and babies. Instead,

157

someone says, "Can I take those bows and ribbons for you and make one of those cute bouquets with the bows as flowers and ribbons pulled through a paper plate? It's kind of corny but I know your affinity for recycle/re-use/ re-purpose, and you'd be set for bows for all the upcoming holidays." The betrothed couple exchanges a look of relief that the "baby topic" has not been thrown into a public forum; and the bride-to-be gratefully hands over the bows and ribbons to be made into a recyclable bouquet.

THE NEWLYWEDS
The question every newlywed hears, "So when are you guys having kids?"

The re-write: A newly-married person bumps into a friend and hears, "Hey! How are you? How's your spouse? How's your job? How's your brother, mother, dog, cat, etc.?" There are so many topics to touch upon when we encounter a friend. When we shed the assumption that every person wants parenthood, only then will the paradigm shift.

THE PLATITUDE
A very popular, powerful script: Children are the ultimate celebration of life!

The re-write: Reaching your potential is the ultimate celebration of life! If you feel that children are a part of that, so be it. For some people, seeing a diversity of wildlife, unthreatened by human activities, is the ultimate celebration of life – a world with clean air and water. For others, getting out of bed in the morning knowing that one's day is one's own is the ultimate celebration of life. Still others feel that the ultimate celebration of life is lack of subjugation by unjust practices/social systems because of one's ethnicity, gender, sexual orientation, ability, age, religious belief, or social status/class/caste.

158

Mahatma Gandhi said:

"If we could change ourselves, the tendencies in the world would also change. As a man changes his own nature, so does the attitude of the world change towards him...We need not wait to see what others do."

When we make a change in ourselves, in what we say and how we react to those around us, then others will begin to change also. Personal actions can come first; and then social change can follow. In the words of cultural anthropologist Margaret Mead, "Never believe that a few caring people can't change the world; for, indeed, that's all who ever have."

The re-writing of scripts is a vast topic. When a woman signs on for motherhood, she should expect to be beamed up to the Mother Ship, where she will be surrounded by little aliens who do not know our language, manners, mores, taboos; they don't know how to forage for food in a strange land; and it takes years before they reach equilibrium, after which they will oscillate between uneven behaviors (e.g., terrible twos, adolescence), taking years to balance out. Once you're a member of the Mother Ship crew, choose your forums for commiseration carefully. Because quite frankly, people without children get a little tired of hearing about the alien invasion.

Likewise, I have heard negative scripts used by the "childfree," laced with vitriol, using words such as "breeders" and their "spawn." Some of this is to be expected among people who feel marginalized by society and prodded by loved ones. A script I could personally do without is being called a Martyr simply because I'm a mom. Viewing a woman through the lens of motherhood is unfair no matter which way the lens is aimed. Again, this is not to say that some mothers don't play the part of

Martyr, but this also is a stereotype. The point of
re-writing the scripts is to do away with stereotypes.

There are some golden rules that can guide our scripts
when speaking to others. Such as, if you don't have
something good to say, don't say anything at all. And, treat
others as you would like to be treated.

The scripts we use with all people, whatever their life
situation, should reflect respect for the integrity of diversity
and equality. Let the slates in our minds, which have been
written upon by others as well as etched by our own
experiences, consider that the slates of others have their
own writings. Sometimes listening and agreeing to
disagree is the most respectful outcome possible.

Perhaps author Richelle Goodrich said it best, "You may
not know my reasons, but you can assume I have
them...and be kind."

"Your assumptions are your windows on the world.
Scrub them off every once in a while or the
light won't come in."
Isaac Asimov, professor of biochemistry

Conclusion: The Vanishing Conversation

Women have been elected to Congress, to the boards of
major corporations, and have flown on space shuttle
missions. Despite all that has changed for women over the
past few decades, the majority of females still grow up
hearing that their ultimate goal is to become mothers.
Motherhood Catechism reinforces this belief by teaching
that a woman's life is less meaningful if she foregoes
motherhood; and it does not elucidate the choices that go
out the window once she becomes a mom. Any allusions to
vanishing choices are downplayed in importance, and seem
to trump other goals she might envision. That motherhood
comes with some extreme sacrifices is also downplayed,
and those sacrifices are exalted as the most selfless
endeavor for a woman's life. In Motherhood Catechism,
the reality that *not* every female will want to, should, or be
able to become a mother is unacknowledged.

The unintended consequences of Motherhood Catechism
include women who clamor for a path they may be better
off not pursuing; for women who never find their way to
the motherhood path, many are left feeling bereft of
enthusiasm for other pursuits; and some women turn their
backs on those who push and prod them toward a path they
are not passionate about, or pales in comparison to another.
It is the rare compassionate person who *intends* to alienate
women without children or push a woman toward a goal
they don't want. But this can happen when the scripts
many of us grew up with go unquestioned without
realization of their impact.

If society were to stop telling females what their lives "should" look like, then perhaps our daughters, sisters, and friends would stop chasing a goal that is unattainable for some or unappealing or damaging for others. Treating all women as though they should fit into some sort of "motherhood mold" can set them up for futures of confusion, depression, and sometimes anger at a world that reminds them that they don't fit in.

Women's ambivalence about motherhood is far from new. They have expressed conflicted feelings about motherhood for centuries; however, the discussion has ebbed and flowed as a women's rights issue. Complicating matters has been the vast difference between the rights of white and black women, with black women embroiled in an additional struggle—one for equal rights based on ethnicity.

Despite past conversations about motherhood as a true choice, and the reality that some women are not drawn to it, women's voices continue to be stifled in the 21st century. Sadly, some of the most important women who toiled to bring these conversations to the forefront are little known figures in history. We must ask ourselves why their voices keep vanishing from mainstream consciousness.

Simone de Beauvoir wrote in her 1949 book, *The Second Sex,* "The child as the supreme aim of woman is a statement having precisely the value of an advertising slogan…The bearing of maternity upon the individual life, regulated naturally in animals by the estrus cycle and the seasons, is not definitely prescribed in woman—society alone is the arbiter."[1]

Tillie Olsen wrote in her 1965 book, *Silences,* "More than in any other human relationship, overwhelmingly, motherhood means being instantly interruptible,

162

responsive...The very fact that these are real needs, that one feels them as one's own...gives them primacy. It is distraction, not meditation, that becomes habitual; interruption, not continuity...Work interrupted, deferred, relinquished, makes blockage—and at best, lesser accomplishment."[2] Olsen was writing about her quest to be a writer; however, her sentiments can be applied to any craft or career a woman may desire. Eventually, Olsen found time to write. During 20 years of raising her children, she said "Writing, or the hope of it, was the air I breathed...and it is no accident that the first work I considered publishable began: 'I stand here ironing...'"

Elisabeth Mann-Borghese was one of few women who questioned a fundamental equality question in her day. In 1936, after being sent to a psychiatrist for help in getting over a love affair, she revealed her ambition to become a great musician; and her analyst told her she needed to choose between her art and family life ("fulfillment as a woman" is how it was phrased). Elisabeth asked, "Why must I choose?" Olsen wrote about Elisabeth's dilemma: that there can be justice only where there is free choice; and injustice will reign where "it is forced because of the circumstances for the sex into which one is born—a choice men of the same class do not have to make in order to do their work."

Women who came of age in the 1960s were well versed on feminist topics; and many denounced the idea that a woman's happiness and identity required suppressing her own desires and interests. With measures such as the Equal Pay Act, legalization of the birth control pill (allowing women to pursue education and careers unpunctuated by unplanned pregnancies), and other women's rights advances, the feminist roar died down in the ensuing decades and motherhood returned to its previous place of reverence. This is not to say that mothers are not to be revered; however, to exalt motherhood as supreme to all other callings is a reversal of the work of previous generations of women, it does not reflect the reality for many women, and it is an attempt at a universal definition of what it means to be female.

There is much that lies below the surface that influences women's lives. In many cases, opting out of motherhood is one of the bravest, least selfish choices a woman can make. To label her dysfunctional or tell her that she's missing out on the quintessential, unparalleled female experience is a grievous injustice.

In the spirit of Plato's *Republic*, can we envision a version of social justice where no female is judged as "less than" because she is not a mother?[3] Although the context of Plato's utopian world is rooted in politics, his ideology was one of individual justice and a cessation of stronger elements of society inducing others into assimilation.

As visionaries for young women, parents can help their daughters keep open minds about their futures by refraining from making assumptions and setting up expectations that may go unmet later in their lives. For those who hold the expectation of becoming grandparents someday, they must ask themselves if holding that expectation is fair and reasonable. One may desire grandparenthood, but does that desire equate to a mandate?

What if your daughter doesn't want to have a child? What if, because of her disinterest, she endures years of intrusive comments or judgment? What if your daughter cannot biologically have a child and utters the words, "What's life about then? Life's not worth living." Or what if she never finds the right situation or resources in which to have a child? Without a mate and not wanting solo motherhood, should she pursue this goal because she's grown up hearing that motherhood is the true expression of womanhood and the ultimate form of love?

The message for women should *not* be "to not have children." Rather, it is to think about what becoming a mother means and to weigh one's options carefully. Honest dialogue is so important when it comes to talking about motherhood. Females need to hear messages of openness and encouragement to choose their own paths. They also need to hear accurate information about sexual health. The sheer mass of inaccurate information (a.k.a. urban legends) about conception is alarming, among teens *and* adults.

Motherhood should *not* be viewed as a mandate, or as integral to a meaningful life. For there are many versions of happiness and fulfillment; and many ways to honor family values.

We need a paradigm shift where society not just accepts, but *encourages*, females to define for themselves what goals are important to them. We must emphasize the importance of what we say to females in their formative years, and dispense with outdated scripts. Of equal importance are messages women continue to hear into adulthood (e.g., no matter how successful they are in their careers, people ask when they're getting married and having kids). I have used revised scripts with friends and associates such as, "*If* your daughter becomes a mom someday…," and the reactions I've received are palpable. Most people are *not* used to hearing motherhood spoken of in this manner. But it's time for that to change.

Robert Fulghum wrote in his book, *All I Really Need to Know I Learned in Kindergarten,* "When we go out into the world, hold hands and stick together."[4] This is a good rule to live by. Supporting each other is such a fundamental ideal, but it seems to get lost amongst the controversy of how women should live their lives. Too often, women let the topic of motherhood (or nonmotherhood) relegate them to opposite sides of the demarcation line. Wouldn't it be great if all women stood together, hand-in-hand, spanning the demarcation line by respecting each other's choices?

Writers have brought about changes in history. Harriet Beecher Stowe's *Uncle Tom's Cabin* was an impetus for the end of slavery. Elizabeth Packard brought about the Packard Laws, protecting women's rights. Kate Chopin's *The Awakening* envisioned different life choices for women at a time when it was unheard of to do so. Betty Friedan and Gloria Steinem started a women's movement that is still evolving today. I do not liken my writings to those of Stowe, Packard, Chopin, Friedan, or Steinem. However, I do endeavor to create a ripple in the sea of society so that every person considers the idea that there is so much more to womanhood than being a mother; and that motherhood is *not* for every woman.

Just as there are two sides to every coin, there are two sides to every issue. Refraining from viewing all females as "future moms" simply allows one to examine both sides of the motherhood coin. It opens up the discussion of motherhood as a true choice rather than a foregone conclusion, and encourages women to pursue authentic lives.

"Numb"
Linkin Park, rock band

Epilogue

I began this book with my daughter in mind. She was 13 at the time; she'll turn 17 by the time this book comes out. It is her voice in the "Aspiring Daughter" segment in Chapter 17. She was about 12 when she talked about being a writer so that she could combine a career with mothering. And I did give her the "re-write" response. I told her of my experiences caring for my kids full-time, and encouraged her to be a writer if that's what she really wanted. I wasn't writing this book at the time of that exchange, so she wasn't emulating my artistry. She was engaged in the "design process" for a career choice based on the assumption that she'd be a mom someday.

Whether this book has an impact on my daughter's future decisions remains to be seen. What I *have* observed is her open-minded approach to this topic. When she overheard fellow female students at her high school pitying an unmarried, childless teacher, her mind shouted, "No! This woman is not to be pitied. She's probably happy and at peace with her life." Her countenance was serious and thoughtful when she recounted this story.

I look upon my daughter's resistance to *assume* whether or not a woman has lived a happy life without motherhood as an application of critical thinking skills. I don't know what my daughter's life will look like in 20 years. I don't *assume* to know. I hope she'll be happy and at peace, whatever her life looks like.

While my inspiration for writing this book began with my daughter, some of what I've written applies to my sons.

Parents hold so much power through the words they use with their children. Men feel expectations emanating from their parents and society, as women do. As with females, we need to respect their journey and support them.

When my oldest son was 10, he announced, "I'm never having kids." I hadn't realized he had overheard me and my husband talking about expenses from a recent vacation. The dollar amount dwarfed the money my son had earned at his lemonade stand the previous summer; he was viewing Mount Everest from his little ant hill. Upon realization that my son was voicing concern about how much having kids costs, I explained that the vacation expenses wasn't as large as it sounded since both my husband and I worked. My son and I had our own separate "aha" moments (and I chastised myself for discussing adult topics within earshot of my kids).

Several years after college, my son once again expressed ambivalence about parenthood. Having lost his job during the Great Recession, he held three part-time jobs simultaneously to make ends meet. At 30, he has a hefty college loan, a condo mortgage, and has faced some tough situations in the form of a fire without adequate insurance (displaced from his home for almost a year), and a major medical expense. Once again, my son is viewing Mount Everest from the auspices of his ant hill.

Today's generation of young adults faces a much different world. It is so much harder to grab a piece of the American dream due to a very different economy than a few decades ago.

My sons' generation grew up hearing that they could be whatever they want to be; that they could follow their dreams, and all would be well. The world they found in their 20s has been inhospitable compared to the visions they held growing up. The truth is that my sons come from a lower middle-income family. And a broken one at that. Their lives are different than what they may have expected when they were younger.

When my oldest son was in college, he put together a final project for his video-editing class, and used Linkin Park's song, *Numb*, in the background. It seemed a hint of things to come. I listened closely to the lyrics that expressed the pressures of trying to be what parents expect their kids to be, of feeling "numb" from the expectations that swirled around them. My son was stretched thin, emotionally and financially, back then and he still is. Who am I to tell him what his life "should" look like?

Chapter 5's epigraph is a letter from my oldest son. I have *always* believed in him, and I'll continue to do so no matter what path his life takes.

I will *always* be a cheerleader for all three of my kids, no matter what "happy" looks like to them. One thing for sure, they'll each chart their courses, and live with the results way beyond my days on Earth. My job is to love and accept them; it's really that simple.

NOTES

Foreword
1. Douthat, Ross. "Parental Pity Party." *The New York Times.* 15 February 2014.

Chapter 2
1. Devlin, Kate. "Marriage without children the key to bliss." *The Telegraph.* Telegraph Media Group, 9 May 2008. Web. <www.telegraph.co.uk/news>
2. Valenti, Jessica. Why Have Kids? A New Mom Explores the Truth About Parenting and Happiness. Las Vegas. Amazon. 2012.
3. Notkin, Melanie. "The Truth about the Childless Life." *Psychology Today.* 12 August 2013. Web. www.pschologytoday.com
4. Martinez, Daniels, Chandra. "Fertility of Men and Women Aged 15-44 years old in the U.S.: National Survey of Family Growth 2006-2010." *National Health Statistics Report.* Number 51. 12 Apr 2012.
5. Knox, Richard. "The Teenage Brain: It's Just Not Grown up yet." NPR.org. 1 March 2010.
6. Poll conducted Sept.-Oct. 2013, St. Xavier University and Elgin Community College.
7. Maslow, Abraham. The Farther Reaches of Human Nature. New York. Viking Press, 1971.
8. Nobelprize.org: The Official Web Site of the Nobel Prize. Web. <www.nobelprize.org>

Chapter 3
1. Brudnick, Manning. "Women of the United States Congress 1917-2014." 18 Feb. 2014. Internet. <www.crs.gov>
2. The Library of Congress: American Memory. "Married Women's Property Laws." Web. <http://memory.loc.gov>

3. "Breaking New Ground – African American Senators." Internet. <www.senate.gov>

4. Sapinsley, Barbara. The Private War of Mrs. Packard. New York. Paragon House, 1991. P.57-63.

5. Sittenfeld, Curtis. "Yes Virginia." *The New York Times.* 20 November 2005. A book review of *Virginia Woolf: An Inner Life* by Julie Briggs. <www.nytimes.com>

6. *Women in History.* Biography on Carrie Chapman Catt. Web. <www.lakewoodpubliclibrary.org>

7. Pilpel, Harriet. "The Right of Abortion." As quoted by <www.womenshistory.com> *Atlantic Magazine,* June 1969.

8. Arthur, Joyce. *Humanist in Canada.* No. 90, Autumn 1989. Discussion of biblical passages that approach the status of the fetus:
Exodus 21:22:25: *"When men strive together, and hurt a woman with child, so that there is miscarriage, and yet no harm follows, the one who hurt her shall be fined according as the woman's husband shall lay upon him; and he shall pay as the judges determine. If any harm follows, then you shall give life for life, eye for eye, tooth for tooth, hand for hand, foot for foot, burn for burn, wound for wound, stripe for stripe. "* This passage allows for the punishment of a man who injures a woman causing her to miscarry. Careful scrutiny of these verses shows that a miscarriage was punishable by a fine; but if death of the woman was caused, the penalty was "a life for a life." The implication of this passage is that the life of the unborn child was not accorded the same status as the life of the woman.
Ecclesiastes 11:5: *"As you do not know how the spirit comes to the bones in the womb of a woman with child, so you do not know the work*

of God who makes everything." This passage speaks of understanding God's ways and will as something unknowable. Interpretation of the Bible can be highly controversial. The **Sixth Commandment,** "Thou shalt not kill," can be up for interpretation when facing war or the death penalty; in the Bible itself, God condemns to death "*all the first-born in the land of Egypt*" (**Exodus 11:4-5**); and in **Psalms 137:8**: God says, "O daughter of Babylon, you devastator! Happy shall he be who takes your little ones and dashes them against the rock!"

9. "Should Our Abortion Laws Be Liberalized?" *Kingsport Times News*. 22 October 1967. Web. <http://newspaperarchive.com/kingsport-times-news/1967-10-22/page-58>

10. As quoted by www.famous.quotes.me.uk, "After Being Convicted of Voting in 1872 Presidential Election: Famous Speech by Susan B. Anthony."

11. "Margaret Sanger Quotes." Web. *Womenshistory.about.com.*

12. "Planned Parenthood at a Glance." PPFA services 5 million worldwide each year. Nearly 3 million women and men in the U.S. annually visit PPFA health centers. 82% of PPFA U.S. health center services are for ages 20 and up.

13. Friedan, Betty. The Feminine Mystique. New York. Norton, 1963.

14. "The 1960s-70s American Feminist Movement: Breaking Down Barriers for Women." *Tavaana.* 2013. Web. <http://tavaana.org>

15. "Single Mom's Fact Sheet." *CoAdobe.org.* Web. <www.coadobe.org/factsheet.php>

Chapter 4

1. Domhoff, G. William. "Who Rules America? Power in America: Wealth, Income and Power."

Updated October 2012. Web. <www2.ucsc.edu/
whorulesamerica/power/wealth.html>
2. Gilbert, Elizabeth. Committed: A Love Story.
New York. Penguin Group, 2010.
3. Strand, Sarah. Amazon review of Two is Enough.
18 August 2011. Web. <www.amazon.com>

Chapter 5
1. Gilligan, Lyons, Hammer. Making Connections.
Cambridge, MA/London. Harvard University
Press, 1990.

Chapter 6
1. Woodruff, Virgina. "These are not My Beautiful
Children." *Brain, Child.* May 2014. Web.
<www.brainchildmag.com/2014/05/these-are-not-my-
beautiful-children>
2. Livingston, G.; Cohn, D. "Childlessness Up Among
All Women; Down Among Women With Advanced
Degrees." *Pew Research Center.* 25 June 2010.
Web. <www.pewsocialtrends.org>
3. Frankl, Victor E. Man's Search for Meaning.
Boston: Beacon Press, 1959. P. 145.
4. Ephron, Delia. Sister Mother Husband Dog: Etc.
New York: Penguin Group, 2013. P. 137.
5. Mosle, Sara. "Parents Make Better Teachers."
Slate.com; The Slate Group, a Division of the
Washington Post Company. 30 August 2013.
Web. <www.slate.com>
6. Cain, Madelyn. The Childless Revolution: What It
Means to be Childless Today. Reading, MA:
Perseus, 2001. P.86.
7. Maslow, Abraham. Motivation and Personality.
New York. Harper & Row, 1954.
8. Wilson, Ruth A. "Belonging." *Exchange
Magazine.* May/June 2012. Web.

9. *Oprah's Angel Network.* Web.
   <http://www.oprah.com/ pressroom/Oprah-
   Winfreys-Official-Biography/6>
10. *BBC News.* "Oprah Winfrey: It's Good to Talk."
    20 November 2009. Web. <http://news.bbc.co.uk/>

Chapter 7
   1. Patton, Susan. <u>Marry Smart: Advice for Finding
      THE ONE</u>. New York. Gallery Books/Simon &
      Schuster, 2014
   2. Sandberg, Sheryl. <u>Lean In For Graduates.</u> New
      York. Alfred A. Knopf/Random House, 2014.
   3. Craig, Amanda. "If Maeve Binchy had been a
      Mother..." *The Telegraph.* 3 August 2012.
      <www.telegraph.co.uk>
   4. Harrington, Van Deusen, Mazar. "The New Dad:
      Right at Home." *The Center for Work & Family*,
      Carroll School of Management, Boston College,
      2012. Web. <www.bc.edu/content/dam/files/
      centers/cwf/pdf>
   5. "The New Dad: Right at Home." Ibid.
   6. U.S. General Accounting Office, "Women's
      Earnings: Work Patterns Partially Explain
      Difference Between Men's and Women's
      Earnings." GAO-04-35. October 2003.
   7. "Wage Gap Statistically Unchanged." *National
      Committee on Pay Equity.* Web. <http://www.pay-
      equity.org>
   8. "Women in Management: Female Managers'
      Representation, Characteristics, and Pay."
      U.S. Government Accountability Office.
      28 September 2010.

Chapter 8
   1. Alcorn, Katrina. <u>Maxed Out: American Moms on
      the Brink</u>. Berkeley. Seal Press, 2013.

2. Williams, Joan and Boushey, Heather. "The Three Faces of Work-Family Conflict." *Center for American Progress (supported by the Ford Foundation and the Rockefeller Family Fund)*. 25 January 2010. Web. <www.americanprogress.org>

3. Thompson, Derek. "Where Did all the Workers Go? 60 Years of Economic Change in 1 Graph." *The Atlantic*. 26 January 2012. Web.

4. "Key Characteristics of Parental Leave Systems." Table PF2.1.A: Full Time Equivalent of Paid Maternity, Paternity, & Parental Leave, 2011. Web. Last updated 10 Oct. 2012. <www.oecd.org>

5. Williams and Boushey. "The Three Faces of Work-Family Conflict. Ibid 2 above.

6. Ibid.

7. Martin, Renee. "Black Women, Feminism and the Ever Popular 'Mommy Wars.'" *Clutchmagonline.com*. 6 May 2012.

8. Steiner, Leslie Morgan. Mommy Wars. *Essay by Sydney Trent: What Goes Unsaid.* New York. Random House, 2007. Pp. 121-123.

9. Warner, Judith. Perfect Madness: Motherhood in the Age of Anxiety. New York. Riverhead Books/Penguin Group, 2005.

10. Sandberg, Sheryl. Lean In: Women, Work, and the Will to Lead. New York. Alfred A. Knopf/ Random House, 2013.

11. Meers, Sharon and Strober, Joanna. Getting to 50/50: How Working Parents Can Have it All by Sharing it All. New York. Bantam Books/Random House, 2009.

Chapter 9
1. "Dan Quayle versus Murphy Brown." *Time Magazine*. June 1, 1992.

2. "Poverty Rate Hits 18-year High as Median Income Falls." MSNBC.com. 13 September 2011. Web. <www.census.gov/newsroom/releases/archives/income_wealth/cb11-157.html>

3. Edin, Kathryn, and Kefalas, Maria. Promises I Can Keep: Why Poor Women Put Motherhood Before Marriage. Berkeley/Los Angeles. University of California Press. 2005. (As quoted in Seeing Ourselves: Classic, Contemporary, and Cross-cultural Readings in Sociology. 7th Ed. 2007. Pp. 66-71.

4. With regard to the $3.3 billion sperm donor industry, "The Anonymous Us Project," founded by Alana Newman, gives voice to the children, now young adults, who are the products of the donor-conception industry. According to Newman, "Despite all best intentions, and being deeply wanted by my mother...I felt like a science experiment." In the case of the fertility clinic owner who fathered 500 to 1,000 children, one of his progeny is Barry Stevens. Stevens said, "Many people say we shouldn't question how we were conceived because we wouldn't otherwise exist." Having that number of half-siblings is unsettling. References: "Get over it: Children of anonymous sperm donors met with hostility, ridicule, say activists." LifeSiteNews.com. 19 June 2012. Web. <www.lifesitenews.com> and Anonymous Us Project. Web. <http://anonymousus.org>

5. Bronfenbrenner, Urie. The Ecology of Human Development. New York. Dover, 1979: P.7.

6. Waldfogel, Craigie, Brooks-Gunn. "Fragile Families and Child Well-being." Vol. 20. No. 2. Fall 2010. Web. <http://futureofchildren.org>

Chapter 10
1. Leonard, Elizabeth. "Mariel Hemingway: Breaking Her Family's Curse." *People Magazine.* 18 November 2013. Pp. 87-90.
2. Burns, Lauri. Punished for Purpose. Livermore, CA. WingSpan Press, 2010.
3. Mamma Mia. Universal Picture, 2008. Movie.
4. Morton, J., Barras, J.R., MacLeod, K. Dear Daddy. Interview with Janetta Rose Barras. Washington, D.C. IYago, 2011. Video.
5. Interviews. Ibid.
6. Jayson, Sharon. "Same-sex couples can be effective parents, researchers find." *USAToday.* 21 Jan. 2010. Web. <www.usatoday.com>

Chapter 11
1. Waldfogel, Craigie, Brooks-Gunn. "Fragile Families and Child Wellbeing." Vol. 20. No. 2. Fall 2010. Web. <http://futureofchildren.org>
2. Clinton, Hillary. It Takes a Village. New York. Simon, 1996. Audio book.
3. Barlow, Rich. "Gay Parents as Good as Straight Ones." *BU Today; Boston University.* 11 April 2013. Web. <www.bu.edu>
4. Perrin, Siegel. "Promoting the Well-Being of Children Whose Parents are Gay or Lesbian." *Official Journal of the American Academy of Pediatrics.* 20 March 2013. Web. <http://pediatrics.aappublications.org>

Chapter 12
1. "Report: Childcare Costs Top Public Four-year Universities in 35 States." *Association of Public & Land-grant Universities.* Study issued by ChildCare Aware America. 16 August 2012.
2. USDA, News Release No. 0241.11. 9 June 2011.

3. USDA, "Expenditures on Children by Families, 2009." Misc. Publication No. 1528-2009. June 2010.
4. "Parents Rationalize the Economic Cost of Children by Exaggerating Their Parental Joy." 2 March 2011. Web. <www.sciencedaily.com>
5. Gilbert, Daniel. Stumbling Upon Happiness. Knopf Doubleday, Inc., 2007. Audio book.
6. "Why Your First Marriage has a 50 Percent Chance of Lasting." *LiveScience*. March 23, 2012. Web. <www.foxnews.com/health/2012/03/23/why-your-1st-marriage-has-50-percent-chance-lasting>
7. Glembocki, Vicki. "Do Kids Cause Divorce?" *Philadelphia Magazine.* August 2010. Web. <www.phillymag.com/articles/do-kids-cause-divorce>

Chapter 13
1. Twenge, Jean. Generation Me. New York. Free Press, 2006. Pp.23-26. And "Jean Twenge Quotes" in ThinkExist.com Quotations Online.
2. Center for Disease Control & Prevention. "Unintended Pregnancy Prevention." 4 April 2012. Web. <www.cdc.gov/reproductivehealth/unintendedpregnancy/>
3. Bedsider.org. Web. <http://bedsider.org/about_us>
4. The Alpha Center. "Facts About Teen Sex." <www.alphacenter-sc.org/teenfacts.php>
5. "Teen Pregnancy Declines, But U.S. Still Lags." *NPR*. 19 August 2012.
6. "Pregnancy and Childbearing Among U.S. Teens." Planned Parenthood Federation of America Fact Sheet. December 2012.
7. "Girls Need Just-in-case Birth Control Prescriptions, Pediatrics Group Says." NBC News staff and wire services. 26 Nov. 2012.

8. "FDA approves Plan B One-Step emergency contraception without a prescription for women 15 years and older." 30 April 2013. <www.fda.gov>

9. Boston Women's Health Book Collective. <u>Our Bodies Ourselves</u>. Simon & Schuster, 2011.

10. Bedsider.org <http://bedsider.org/about_us>

11. Planned Parenthood

12. Women's Capital Corporation. <www.planbonestep.com/pharmacylocator.aspx>

13. Supreme Court of the United States. "Secretary of Health & Human Services, et al, v. Hobby Lobby Stores, Inc. 30 June 2014.

14. "U.S. Religious Landscape Survey." *Pew Forum.* Web. <http://religions.pewforum.org/pdf/table-children-by-tradition.pdf>

15. Stacey, Dawn. "What Do Religions Say About Birth Control and Family Planning?" Web. <http://contraception.about.com>

16. "The Use of Contraception in the United States: 1982 to 2008." Published 2010 by U.S. Department of Health and Human Services - Centers for Disease Control and Prevention.

17. HHS v Hobby Lobby Amicus Brief 13-354. 21 October 2013.

18. Trussell, James, PhD, and Raymond, Elizabeth, MD. "Emergency Contraception: A Last Chance to Prevent Unintended Pregnancy." October 2013. Web. <ec.princeton.edu/questions/ec-review.pdf> As quoted by The National Campaign to Prevent Teen & Unplanned Pregnancy: "Weight, what?" 10/31/13. Web. <blog.thenationalcampaign.org>

19. Planned Parenthood – abortion laws in states

20. "Parents and Teens Talk about Sexuality: A National Poll." Poll conducted on behalf of Planned Parenthood, Family Circle, and the Latino Adolescent & Family Health Center at NYU. June 2012. Web. <http://plannedparenthood.org>

21. Lindemann, Charles, PhD. "Mechanisms of Sperm Motility." Undated (originally published in Fall 2010 issue of The Oakland Journal). Web. <www2.oakland.edu/biology/lindemann/spermfacts.htm>

Chapter 14
1. McBridge, Karyl, Ph.D. "The Six Faces of Maternal Narcissism." *Psychology Today.* 14 March 2011. Web. <www.psychologytoday.com>

Chapter 15
1. On-line Thesaurus: One antonym for "mother." *2013 Dictionary.com LLC* Web. Accessed on 4 November 2013. <http://thesaurus.com>
2. Brown, Genevieve Shaw. "Mommy Wars: Moms Team Up to End the Breast vs. Formula Fight." *ABCNew.go.com.* Web. <http://abcnews.go.com>
3. Graham, Barbara (editor). Eye of My Heart: 27 Writers Reveal the Hidden Pleasures & Perils of being a Grandmother. New York. Harper, 2009.
4. Meier, Joyce. "The Refusal of Motherhood in African American Women's Theater." University of Michigan, Ann Arbor. *MELUS.* Autumn-Winter 2000.
5. Collins, Patricia Hill. Black Feminist Thought: Knowledge, Consciousness, and the Politics of Empowerment. New York. Routledge, 2000.
6. Gilbert, Elizabeth. Committed: A Love Story. U.S.A. Penguin, 2010. Pp. 230-233.
7. Commencement Address by Stephanie Mills. Mills College, Oakland, California. *Mills Quarterly.* August 1969. Web. <http://www.mills.edu/news/2009/MillsCommencementSpeech1969.pdf>

Chapter 16
1. Moore, Suzanne. "Having or Not Having Children Should Not Define or Divide Women." *The Guardian.* 15 January 2014.

Chapter 17
1. O'Brien Hallstein, D. Lynn. Contemplating Maternity in an Era of Choice: Explorations of Discourses of Reproduction. U.S.A. Rowman & Littlefield, 2010. P. 23.
2. Kamma, Anne. If You Lived when Women Won Their Rights. U.S.A. Scholastic, Inc. 2008.

Conclusion
1. Beauvoir, Simone de. The Second Sex. New York. Alfred A. Knopf, Inc., 1952.
2. Olsen, Tillie. Silences. New York. Feminist Press, 2003. First copyright by Tillie Olsen 1965. Pp. 19, 31.
3. Plato. The Republic. Written approx. 380 B.C. Translation by Robin Waterfield. Oxford University Press: 1993.
4. Fulghum, Robert. All I Need to Know I Learned in Kindergarten. Random House: 1986.

Made in the USA
Las Vegas, NV
01 March 2022

44829562R00115